Light Through Stained Glass

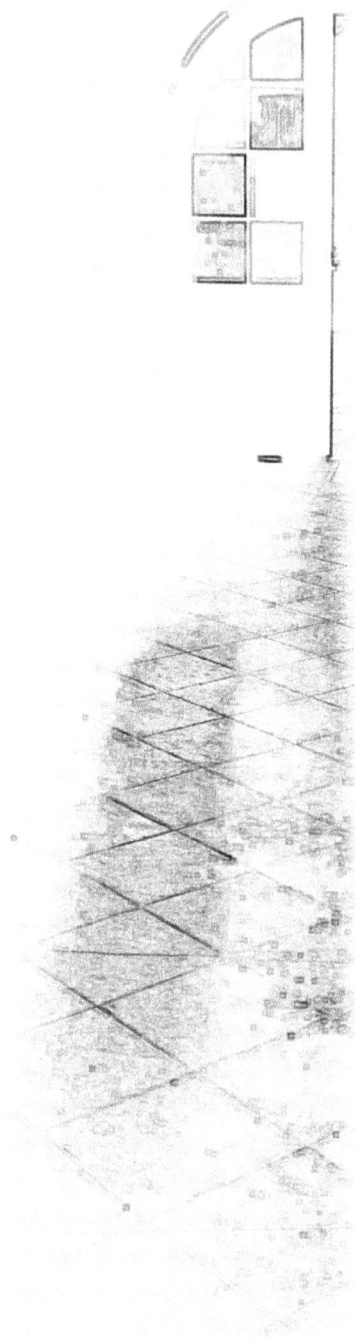

Dr. Richard E. Blackwell

Library of Congress Control Number: 2010909341
ISBN: Hardcover   978-1-4535-2675-0
        Softcover   978-1-4535-2674-3

Much of this work is fiction and based on fictional characters.
Surnames are fictional in that portion of the work that is based
on real life ministerial experiences of the author.

This book was printed in the United States of America.

To order additional copies of this book, contact:
Xlibris Corporation
1-888-795-4274
www.Xlibris.com
Orders@Xlibris.com
59942

I dedicate this book to Dr. Donald Brash, superb scholar, excellent professor, and good friend.

I must also express appreciation to my wife Linda for her excellent editing and book design and to my daughter Ashley for cover design and art.

All three of these special people encouraged me to publish this collection of short stories.

Contents

Margie

The week had been a long one, a week filled with problems large and small. Saturday, my usual day off, was filled with both a funeral and a wedding. As a pastor, I looked forward with delight to a day of rest so that I could be at my best on Sunday morning; but this was not to be. Not that I would be another Spurgeon, Graham, or Dunham if I had enough rest; but I could at least offer my sermon with clarity, drive, and care. Perhaps I was feeling a bit sorry for myself as the week ended. Alas, I have rather large clay feet.

Saturday morning came with the sound of pouring rain, which had also been true of Friday as well. The local weatherman said that an occluded front had stalled over the area and would not clear away until late Saturday afternoon. Several inches of rain had fallen already with more expected as the day progressed.

My wife heard me get up and saw me looking out the bedroom window. She sleepily commented that it was a bad day for a funeral and a wedding. I grunted, started gathering my clothes, and headed for the shower. It crossed my mind that all I had to do was grab some soap and step outside, but this was quickly challenged by the thought of being arrested for lewd conduct. Now that would please the deacon board.

After completing my bathroom chores, inside the house, I dressed in a dark suit and tie, downed some toast and coffee, and left for the church building to study my funeral sermon and the wedding service.

The wedding was one that I would thoroughly enjoy, because I liked the young couple. They were from all indications a perfect match and a joy to be around. The rehearsal on the previous evening, despite the rain, had gone smoothly with much laughter and cooperation. Even the prospect of rain at the time of the wedding couldn't dampen the spirits of the wedding party. The funeral was another matter.

Funerals are sad enough occasions without complications, but they are deeply disturbing when there is family division and open hostility. Over my years in the pastorate, I had stopped a fistfight in front of a mother's casket, stepped in between sisters fighting about who gets what from their parents' home, mediated arguments over wills, and preached to divided congregations of angry families. The present funeral was a particularly difficult one. The husband and father of the family had deserted his wife and children years before for another woman and her children. The result, as you can imagine, was bitterness and anger in the deserted family; and as he had not sought a divorce from his first wife, the estate was a matter of open emotional and legal warfare between both families. Frankly, I didn't know what to expect at the funeral home or the graveside.

When I entered the chapel of the funeral home, the room was clearly divided with each family sitting sullenly in silence. I delivered the homily and included a call for a thoughtful resolution of the problems that overshadowed a man's death. The chapel emptied in deadly silence, and we went to our cars for the journey to the cemetery. The rain added to the misery by coming down like a waterfall fed by a swollen river.

The cemetery was flooded: water stood in the driveways and around many of the graves. Slowly and carefully, the procession made its way to a tent-covered grave. The workers had done their best with the site, but poor drainage caused water to stand ankle deep around the grave. I led the coffin to the site under the umbrella of one of the directors and took my place at the head of the casket. Both of my shoes were filled with water, and the right side of my suit was drenched. I was miserable to say the least. But my own difficulties paled into insignificance in the shadow of the families' problems. There was some jostling as the families tried to get under the tent to fill the front row of chairs. Finally, the chairs were removed to avoid open conflict. A few people had remained in their cars and were joined by disgruntled persons, unhappy with the arrangements. Neither the funeral director nor I was popular with either family.

After what seemed a prolonged struggle, the director turned to me with a look of relief and asked for the service to begin. I had just started to read the selected scriptures when I heard a woman's voice screeching like fingernails on a blackboard. The racket was so loud that I could not continue. The husband of the woman was dispatched to ascertain the problem, but the irritating voice continued to send out a barrage of vituperations. After what seemed several minutes, I handed my Bible to the director and walked over to the car, leaving behind grumbling and snickers.

"Excuse me, but what is the problem," I asked assertively.

"I didn't want to come, and I want to leave! I want to go shopping! That old bastard should be buried at the dump!" Looking at her husband, she shouted at the top of her lungs, "Get me the hell out of here!"

"Calm down!" I said. "Whatever you think about this man, have some respect for where you are and the people gathered here."

"I want to go shopping . . . I want to go to the mall! Do you hear me?" With that, she gave an angry look at her husband.

"Ma'am, either shut up or shut the window," I said angrily. I turned to her husband and told him to take her to the mall. He got in the car and drove away, trailing the verbal fumes of scatology.

I stood in the cemetery drive, watching the car until it disappeared from my sight. I was angry and drenched and hardly in a mood to read scripture and lead people in prayer. *What kind of person would behave like that at a funeral? Why didn't she just go shopping in the first place, rather than cause a scene?*

I thought. Gathering my composure, I sloshed back to the grave and finished the interment. The families scattered with various inappropriate responses and recriminations at the deceased and at one another. I sat for some time in my car, emotionally exhausted and wet.

Looking at my watch, I realized that I had to get back to the church building. The florist was coming at noon and so was the caterer. There was no time to go home to change clothes, so I would have to dry my suit at the building and try to make it as presentable as possible. Fortunately, I wore a Geneva robe for services, which would cover my unkempt condition.

Driving back to the church, I was still steaming, physically and emotionally, when I came upon a convenience store. *Coffee,* I thought, and quickly drove into the parking lot. I walked back to the bank of coffee pots looking like an overdressed, soaking-wet street urchin. The store was empty except for a young woman at the cash register.

With coffee in hand, I approached the counter. The young woman had light brown hair, frumpy clothes (look who's talking), and a thin, frightened appearance. She had a pleasing appearance, but her eyes looked around furtively, never settling on anything but the cash register. Obviously shy, she extended a necessary amenity and proceeded to ring up the wrong amount.

"Two dollars?" I asked harshly.

"I'm sorry, sir. I made a mistake," she responded quietly without looking at me.

"Look," I said thoughtlessly, "this is a simple transaction. What's the problem?" My voice was dripping with sarcasm and tinged with anger.

The young woman, her nametag said "Margie," turned toward me with tears just beginning to run down her cheeks. "I'm sorry," she said.

I stood there stunned at my own unkindness and bad temper. The anger and frustration left over from the funeral had spilled over Margie like the hot coffee I held. Immediately, I thought of my daughter Ashley and how I would feel if she had received such treatment. "Please, miss, forgive me for my mistreatment of you. I was unkind, and I'm sorry."

She looked at me with surprise and muttered, "It's OK." But her words and facial expression shared more than a passing gesture. It was as if she had no right to expect better, as if her whole life was a morass of humiliation and rejection. Margie brushed the tears from her cheeks and finished the transaction.

Picking up my coffee, I was about to beat a hasty retreat in a fog of embarrassment when I realized that I had to do more. The florist and the caterer would just have to wait a bit.

I turned and walked the few steps back to the counter. "Miss . . . Margie, it's not OK. What I just did is not OK." She looked at me with a bewildered expression on her pretty, but hard, features. She started to speak, but stopped.

I continued, "No one has the right to treat you the way I did. Do you understand?"

Finding the courage to look me right in the eye, she said, "Why should you be different than anyone else?"

"Because you don't deserve such treatment, and I was just taking out my frustration on you. That had nothing to do with you."

"Look, mister, don't worry about it. My old man has been treating me like a dummy all my life," she offered flatly. "I don't know why I cried. I should be used to it by now."

"Margie, you hold a responsible job in this store. This store wouldn't hire a person who couldn't do the job. Money is at stake. No one, and I mean no one, would hire a 'dummy' to handle money!"

Margie grinned, and I turned to leave.

As I sat in my car in the parking lot, I thought about all the young people among us who start life with an acute lack of self-respect; because parents, teachers, peers, and fellow travelers treat them as deserving no respect, as throwaways, or as physical or emotional punching bags. And I had just treated Margie that way! As I drank my coffee, it tasted bitter and just a little salty.

The Failure

It was my day off, and Linda, the children, and I traveled to our hometown, High Point, North Carolina. I was a young pastor in Valdese, located some eighty-five miles west in the foothills of the mountains. The weather was unusually mild for a midsummer day, because a cold front had passed through the previous Sunday, leaving in its wake cloudless blue skies, cool air, and low humidity. Piling into our new American Motors American, we drove south on Eldred Street to Highway 40 east. Spirits were high as we drove along, for we were enjoying our new car. My previous car was a Renault Dauphine, which reduced us to the level of sardines every time we took a trip. Not only so, but the Renault could barely make the highway minimum speed of forty-five miles per hour. Our children laughed and joked as we approached a highway exit, shouting at the top of their lungs that we didn't have to slow down to go onto the ramp. So the new car, coupled with the expectation of visiting our families, produced a joyous atmosphere in our little flivver.

Our first stop in High Point was at Linda's grandparents' home on Ennis Street. After work, Linda's mom came over to join us for an early supper prepared by Mrs. Hammett, Linda's grandmother. Mrs. Hammett was a tall, thin matron of a bygone era. She was a beautiful, high-spirited, bright, and dignified lady with a talent for making the best cornbread I've ever tasted. Mrs. Hammett not only carried herself with grace, but also had a sense of humor that would knock your socks off. It came out of left field when you least expected it and could completely change the atmosphere in a room. When you coupled that sense of humor with a sudden natural chuckle, one quickly realized that a marvelous capacity for life dwelled in this daughter of Alabama.

While the ladies were preparing the table, Mr. Hammett engaged me in discussions of politics, labor issues, gardening, baseball, and about any other topic that could develop into a rousing argument. The old gentleman was remarkable. He was a veteran of WWI, a baseball player, a supervisor in a cotton mill, an excellent gardener, and an armchair philosopher. He stood just over six feet tall, thin, angular, handsome, and dignified. He, like his wife, had a sense of humor; and he had a remarkably keen sense of fair play. Very little got by him, causing him to think deeply about his world and the meaning of life. When Mr. Hammett and I argued, Linda and her grandmother wondered if we were going to come to blows, but we were really enjoying ourselves immensely. We always ended on the best of terms.

On this particular day, I suddenly felt a strong urge to see an old friend, who owned a grocery store on English Street. These kinds of urges have followed me all of my career as a Christian pastor and were always indicative of someone's need. I have never ceased to be amazed by their emergence and the people I was led to help.

I told Linda that I was going to see Mr. Reed and was met with a stern look and a sharp reminder that supper would be ready at five o'clock. I reminded her that it was only four and assured her I'd return by mealtime. As I walked to the car, I couldn't help but note again how beautiful the sky was and how refreshing the air. For a few moments, I just stood on the front walk breathing deeply and rejoicing at being alive.

I drove the short block to Tryon Street, turned left, and a short block later turned right onto Green Street. Ward Street took me to English Street to a local grocery store. I drove past the market to a small parking lot, turned around, drove back to the store, and parked in front. Sitting there, memories flooded my mind, such as crating bottles in the basement, stocking shelves, draying groceries, watering vegetables, and cleaning the meat counter.

Nothing seemed to have changed very much from the time I worked for Reed. The store was a clapboard gray building with a parking lot in the back. The front was screened with heavy steel wire for safe storage of unshelved stock and the delivery bike. Through the middle of this screened front was an entrance with large double doors. As one entered, there was the checkout counter and to the left a large fresh-vegetable counter, and the general merchandise shelves covered the remaining floor space to the meat counter at the back. The store was almost overflowing with merchandise as always, and I looked around to find Reed. He was standing at the vegetable rack, watering down the produce.

I couldn't help but smile when I saw him. He was shorter than I, standing about five feet and eight inches. His face was round with chubby cheeks that glowed with a soft pink color. His eyes were coal black and filled with energy, and his black hair, showing signs of gray, was slicked back under a butcher's cap that was turned sideways. An ample head sat on a bull-like neck, which spread into piston-like arms that exuded power. A round belly filled his butcher's apron and sat sturdily on short but powerful legs. Nothing flabby showed itself, rather a firmness born of hard work. Put him in a green suit and top hat and stick a pipe in his mouth, and he would have looked like an oversized leprechaun. Certainly, his manner would lend credibility to that image. Forceful, opinionated, and hard, Reed was on the surface a difficult man. So I found him when I first worked for him.

Mr. Reed gave me my first chance to work for pay. Oh, I had worked for my Uncle Thedy and my grandfather on their respective farms, but that was expected of me as a young boy. Reed offered me seventy-five cents an hour to dray groceries, stock shelves, and generally clean up after the Saturday rush. The day was ten hours long, and the work was constant. Very few breaks were allowed: business was business. Those Saturdays were a complete bust, because I didn't like Reed's abruptness and unrelenting demand for work. Draying groceries on a bike, with a basket as big as I, was no fun at all. It had one gear, thus making hills impossible when the bike was fully loaded. Walking as much as I rode, I hated draying groceries. Coupled with a multitude of other chores, I felt ill used and underpaid. I quit!

A few years later, after I had grown a bit both physically and emotionally, I returned to work for Reed on a part-time basis. In addition, I had come to appreciate Reed's approach and depth of character. This time I enjoyed working for him and doing what I could to help a failing business. The large supermarkets had just about killed the family-owned stores in High Point, and Reed's store was gradually losing customers to the chains. A comparable situation now exists with the rise of Wal-Mart: mom-and-pop stores are forced out of business. Essentially, I worked for groceries, which helped me to support my young family.

I learned something about Mr. Reed during those years that has remained with me all of my life. This seemingly hard businessman was one of the kindest, sweetest people I've ever known. Time and time again, he let out groceries on credit to poor families, knowing full well that they could never repay him;

and when community need arose, he would step in to assist. One example will suffice from among the many that occurred.

One afternoon, a local neighbor ran into the store to tell us that a family around the corner on Ward Street had been burned out. The family was safe, but they had lost everything in the fire. Without missing a beat, he walked through the store putting groceries in a basket and then sent me to take them to the family, who was staying with a neighbor. He strictly forbade my telling the family the source of the groceries. "Just leave the groceries and come back" were his words. I did just as he instructed. He sought no credit and wanted none. Such were his many acts of generosity to the community. I loved Reed as a son does a father and respected him as a Christian man.

This was the man I approached as I walked over to the vegetable counter.

"Hi, Reed, how are you doing?" I asked with a smile.

"Things are a little slow in the store business," he responded with a grin as he extended his hand.

"I'm sorry, Reed. I had hoped that things would improve."

"How's your family, Dick? I haven't seen them in a while. Don't you have two children, a boy and a girl?"

"Yes, sir, Richie and Ashley," I replied proudly. "They're growing like topsy," I continued. "By the way, how is James? I looked in next door at the insurance office, but he's not there."

"My boy is a big success. He's worked hard to build his business," Reed replied with appropriate pride in his son.

The conversation continued with small talk mostly about customers that I remembered from my days at the store. This went on for several minutes when suddenly Reed said, "I'm pretty tired. I'm thinking about taking some time off."

"You! Taking time off? I can't believe that!" I said with surprise.

"Yeah, I might just take a trip, get away, you know," Reed said with a slight hint of sadness or just tiredness. I wasn't sure.

I looked at my watch and saw that my time was up: I had to get back for supper. Reed wanted to continue our talk, but I had to leave. I reached for his hand, shook it, and said my good-bye. As I walked out of the store, a sadness overtook me, and I didn't feel good about leaving. *I'll be back*, I thought. *In fact, I'll make my next visit very soon.*

Soon I was back at the Hammett's home and enjoying a fine supper and time with our family. Reed quietly slipped away amid laughter and discussion. After supper, I reminded Linda that I had to get back to Valdese, and we started about six thirty, arriving home about dusk.

As the next few days passed, I felt a deep uneasiness, but I didn't know why. Reed came to mind occasionally, and I felt sadness, but nothing more. My thoughts were that a way of life was passing, and Reed had made no real provision to meet a new world that excluded his kind of merchant. More's the pity!

Early one morning, the phone rang; and when that happens in a pastor's home, one expects a serious problem, an emergency. And so it was. My mother-in-law Helen called to tell me that Mr. Reed had committed suicide. All I could do was stutter a response and a mournful "Why?" I heard, without confirmation, that he had been told that the store would be seized. When he couldn't find a source of money, he went into his den early the next morning and shot himself. Apparently, he couldn't face the last day in his beloved store and the last day of a way of life.

When I received the news from High Point, the visit to the store replayed in my mind like a slow-motion film. The conversation was as clear as a crystal, and its meaning leaped at my throat like a garrote. I had been too distracted to hear a friend tell me that he was going to kill himself. I listened, but I didn't hear. I missed its meaning, and nothing in this world could recover that moment and my chance to save a friend. No long time passes without my remembering that day and my friend, and the fact that I was insensitive to another person's life and death struggle.

Thirty or more years have passed since the death of one of the best men I've ever known. That failure which cost a man his life helped to save others along the way, for I was able to step in on several occasions to stop suicides from occurring. From that event, I learned to listen to others when they cried for help. But on that day in that grocery store, I failed. Nothing will ever change that, nothing!

What a shame that we Christians often either shoot our wounded or ignore them. How unlike Jesus is the church at times, for he heard and responded over and over again to cries for help. The state of a person's life mattered not when help was requested: Jesus responded to heal body and soul. Can we who use his name so freely fail to do the same? The worst indictment I can ever contemplate is to hear Jesus ask me, "Why didn't you listen to the little ones when they came to you for help? I listened to you and gave you your life. How could you ignore or dismiss the little ones in my name?"

Something about Lou Gehrig

As I stepped out of the parsonage that Sunday, I was immediately taken in by a beautiful spring morning, clear blue skies, budding trees, and a sweet warmth. Unfortunately, I couldn't stop for very long, because I was on my way to church to lead the morning worship. The basement steps were only a few feet from the parsonage and provided my usual approach to the church building. Quickly walking along the basement hall to the front stairs, I mounted the steps two at a time until I reached the sanctuary. Once there, I looked over the preparations for the morning worship and prepared to meet the early arrivals.

As I stood on the dais looking over the bulletin, Paul, one of our Elders, came rapidly down the center aisle. He was clearly on an important errand.

"Preacher, one of my sons is here from Nashville and is outside. I want you to meet him."

"Lead the way, Paul. I'd very much like to meet him. By the way, which son is he?" I said preparing to greet him.

"Charles," said Paul, "you know, the football player. I mean the one who played for Valdese High School."

"Oh yes," I responded, remembering the stories I had heard about the championship year and some of Charles's exploits on and off the field.

We stepped out of the foyer and on to the steps at the front of the building. I watched with intense interest as Charles, his wife, and little daughter mounted the steps. Charles still looked every bit the athlete of years gone by. Tall, lean, and muscular, he looked as if he could put on a football uniform and enter a game immediately. His wide shoulders and thin waist gave him the appearance of a male model; and his sculptured facial features, blond, crew cut hair, and powerful chin only enhanced that image.

But something seemed amiss as he approached us: his movement seemed unsteady and hesitant. I stretched out my hand ready for a strong handshake, but he took his left hand and picked up his right arm to enable a response. His hand had deteriorated; the muscles, especially about the thumb, seemed almost nonexistent. Observing the look of surprise on my face, he mumbled something about Lou Gehrig; but I was so taken aback that I only realized later that morning the significance of what he had said. He had ALS, "Lou Gehrig's disease" as it is sometimes called, a wasting illness that had killed the *Pride of the Yankees* and now threatened Charles.

My contact with Charles and his family that Sunday was brief, and I only learned the following Sunday of his return to Nashville. From time to time, I inquired of his parents, Paul and Alma, about Charles's condition and about his wife and daughter, but received only sketchy reports in response. Then one day, some months later, Paul told me that Charles had come home to live. The way he said it let me know that Charles was alone and that

I should just accept that fact without question or comment. He did press me to make a visit as soon as possible.

Visiting Charles was not going to be easy for me, for I anticipated an emaciated young man, bereft of family, and preparing to die. When I arrived at the family home, I was greeted matter-of-factly by Paul, so as to avoid unnecessary conversation. The atmosphere was tense and cold. As I entered his room, Charles was seated in a wheelchair. Thinner than when I last saw him, braces now swallowed his once powerful legs; his arms were small, limp, and powerless; and his face was thin and strained. Paul, who had escorted me to Charles's room, invited me to sit down and, wraith-like, slipped from our presence. With a slight jerk of his head and twitch of arms, Charles began to speak, "My wife has taken my daughter and left me. She didn't want to be married to a dying cripple." I sat quietly, knowing that there was much more that he needed to say.

"I can't say that I blame her though. I haven't exactly been a sensitive or caring husband." Tears started from his eyes, but he quickly lowered his face to his hand to wipe them away. "I miss my little girl, and I'm afraid that I'll never see her again. I really don't want anything from my wife, except a chance to see my little girl before I die. But they've moved to Florida, and I don't know how to reach them."

"Charles, I'm sorry for what has happened to you. I don't know how anyone can bear such a devastating reversal of circumstances," I responded with tears in my voice. "I'll do everything I can to help you, but you must tell me what is needed."

"Preacher, I'm being provided for by my parents with help from my brother and sister who live in Nashville. But I would appreciate visits, prayers, and some Bible study."

"Of course, Charles, I'll visit regularly, and I'm sure the congregation will have special prayer times for you."

"I don't want to be a burden to anyone, and my doctors tell me that I have about a year to live. I just don't want to choke to death. You know, that's how many ALS patients die. I don't want to die that way; that's the only thing I'm really afraid of. So tell the church to pray that it won't happen to me."

Stunned by his words, I just sat quietly and waited. He continued.

"I'm a Christian, you know. Oh, I haven't been one for long, but I am now. I've wasted so much time running from God and hurt so many people along the way. My wife, you know, left me because I had hurt her, and I don't blame her for deserting me. I only wish I had known Christ many years ago. I've hurt so many people. I don't think my dad wants me here. Not that he says that, but I can tell. Mom will do anything for me. I love her so much. Preacher, you must know that she is special, a loving Christian lady."

"Yes, Charles, Alma is a truly fine person who has had a very difficult life."

"Tell me about it," said Charles with a hard edge to his voice.

With that, and feeling a little uncomfortable that his father might be listening, I offered to read from the Psalms. I ended with a Psalm of exiled Israel, Psalm 130:

"Out of the depths I cry to you, O Lord.

Lord, hear my voice!

Let your ears be attentive to the voice of my supplications!

If you, O Lord, should mark iniquities, Lord, who could stand?

But there is forgiveness with you, so that you may be revered.

I wait for the Lord, my soul waits,

And in his word I hope;

My soul waits for the Lord more than those who watch for the morning, more than those who watch for the morning.

O Israel, hope in the Lord!

For with the Lord there is steadfast love, and with him is great power to redeem.

It is he who will redeem Israel from all its iniquities."

At the conclusion of the reading, I prayed and started to leave, but Charles stopped me.

"I don't feel the way Israel felt in exile," said Charles. "I feel that my illness has opened my eyes and life to a new world. I'm filled with a joy I've never known before. Preacher, in spite of everything, I'm thankful for God's grace and love."

I was momentarily floored. I stood looking at him as if he were an angel, for mere mortals just don't talk that way. But right in front of me was a physically broken man, transcending everything he faced by means of faith in Christ Jesus. That's when a pastor is humbled and led to examine his own life and faith.

A few months after returning home, Charles and his mother sought out a doctor in North Carolina who treated MS and ALS with heavy doses of vitamins and fresh vegetable juice. The church joined in their search for a cure by holding regular prayer sessions and by making special visits to encourage Charles. His ALS went into remission and remained so for several years. During those years, I was Charles's regular visitor, gradually becoming his close friend. We talked, joked, laughed, cried, and prayed together. Everything was shared, and the trust of bearing the freedom of the other was absolute. When he came to church, the men of the congregation transported Charles in his wheelchair into the sanctuary, just like a pope. Nothing made the church more alive than Charles's presence. All of our lives were enriched spiritually by the undying faith and growing joy that lived in the heart of this physically wrecked man.

Throughout the period of remission, Charles continued to share with me his greatest fear, death by choking. The comments were brief, but deeply disturbing to me, for I remembered my bouts with enlarged tonsils and the awful sensation of choking. Often we prayed together that God would spare Charles such a death.

As the years passed, Charles remained about the same, neither better nor worse. His mother faithfully met his needs, caring for her helpless son as she had when he was an infant. My visits continued.

On a fall afternoon, I arrived as usual and found Charles in a very solemn mood. I knew without a word passing between us that he had started to decline. There had been a change in his strength, in how he could clear his throat, and in how he was able to swallow. His doctors confirmed that ALS had reasserted its deadly power.

Though dreadfully afraid of choking to death, he stopped mentioning it. He seemed resigned to that possibility. During this decline, Charles was finally reunited with his daughter, who brought a brightness to him and a sense of peace as to his daughter's well-being. She was a beautiful, healthy, well-adjusted young lady who loved and missed her father. Their time together was short, but he gave himself to her future and shared his faith with a wonderful gentleness.

Shortly before Easter, Alma called and urged me to come to see Charles immediately. I pulled on my sport coat and drove down Eldred Street. When I arrived, Alma was standing on the front porch looking small and weary, wringing her hands and crying.

"I think, I think, he's dying," she sobbed. "He wants to tell you something."

I rushed into the bedroom and took him in my arms. He wanted to sit up, so I held him against me to support him. Charles turned his head toward me, offering up every ounce of strength left in his body. His breath was terribly shallow and labored, and his words were just a whisper, "It's OK. It's OK." With that he closed his eyes and sank into a coma. His head slid into the notch where my neck and shoulders joined. We remained in that position until the ambulance arrived to transport him to Valdese General Hospital.

Alma approached me just before leaving for the hospital and asked what he had said. I told her. She smiled and said, "He didn't choke to death. Thank God!" Both of us cried out of gratitude for the peaceful way that Charles was departing.

The hospital emergency room staff tried to revive him and in the process intubated him, but the heroic measures were to no avail. He was brain-dead. On the Friday before Easter, Good Friday, the tube was removed, and Charles's struggle ended. I was with the family when they made their last visit with Charles. There was a profound sadness that accompanied great relief. A special man had departed, one who had left behind a legacy of love and faith that cast a shadow of the cross over his earlier life of selfishness and unkindness.

The funeral was on Easter Monday, and I spoke honestly about Charles's life as he had specifically requested. I also spoke of what he had become in Christ Jesus, finding a new life through the death of his body. He was a remarkable example of the human struggle shaped in death by spiritual life.

My final words at the funeral were his favorite. They came from an old Negro Spiritual: "Free at last, free at last! Thank God Almighty, free at last!"

Something about Lou Gehrig had lived in Charles, and it wasn't just ALS. It was the courage and dignity of a man who learned how to live and how to die.

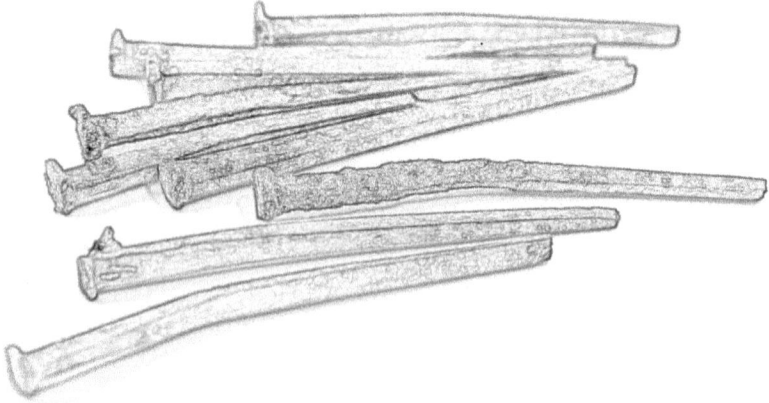

Rusty Nails

Until I was about seven years old, I roamed and played on the east side of Meadow Street, from Ferndale Avenue on the north to English Street on the south. The west side of Meadow Street was a foreign country to me, because I was never allowed to cross the road on my own. My one and only attempt to escape to the greener grass on the other side ended with a paddling issued by Mrs. Nance who was our neighbor and sentry. Her see-all, know-all presence was like having a video cam surveying my every move. *Big Sister* was always watching, or so it seemed.

Within the boundaries set by my parents and Mrs. Nance was a smorgasbord of childhood amusement. Our duplex apartment was located between the

Nances on the left (facing the apartment) and the Chastains on the right. I liked the Nance family, especially the sons, Buddy and Junior, for they were high school students who took the time to befriend and protect the younger kids in the neighborhood. They were mischievous to say the least, but two kinder, more thoughtful young men I have never known. Sometimes I was a source of amusement for them, but never a focus of unkindness. Woody Chastain was my own age, and we explored our domain with the boundless energy of young boys. Woody had reddish-brown hair, a generous supply of freckles, a lean body, and considerable speed for a kid. He had a winsome smile that transfigured his face into sunshine and a laugh that delighted me, something between a rib-splitter and a giggle. We seldom argued or fought, but when we did, it was a lulu. There was the time we decided to disagree by chucking rocks at one another over the backyard fence. My aim, on this occasion, was better and resulted in a piece of cinder splitting Woody's eyebrow open so that it needed several stitches. He got all the glory, and I got all the grief. But the next day, Woody and I were playing as usual. He seemed to appreciate my aim, because he received several gifts to ease his pain and delighted in being able to tell the other kids in the neighborhood what I had done to him.

Down the street toward English, next to the Chastains, lived two old-maid sisters, the Asburys. One of the sisters was a banker and the other a music teacher. Both were kind and generous, especially at Halloween.

The corner property next to the Asburys belonged to the Glovers, old Mr. Glover and his wife. The land at the back of the house and along the sidewalk on Meadow Street was used for a vegetable garden. Woody and I liked the Glovers, because they allowed us to pick tomatoes—not too many, mind you—for snacks on summer afternoons. There was nothing better than a warm vine-ripened tomato as a summer afternoon snack. Woody and I even carried salt in our pockets to flavor them. We also carried worms, bugs, and toads in those pockets that only enhanced the flavor. Woody and I must have ingested enough germs to slowly immunize us against most diseases, for we were seldom sick.

Mr. Glover was something of a local curiosity, for he survived a bout with tetanus, commonly called *lockjaw*. The neighbors and members of a local church held regular prayer vigils and carried in meals to help the Glovers. Woody and I held our own vigil, waiting to see if Mr. Glover's jaw would unlock. We planned to test him by engaging him in conversation as soon as we saw him sitting on the front porch.

My friend and I roamed the neighborhood often, but we spent most of our time in Woody's backyard or mine. His backyard was grassy and good for pitching ball, playing touch football, talking under a shade tree, and wrestling. My backyard was bare earth, not a blade of grass until you reached the Nance property. It was good for digging, building roads, dirt fights, and any number of construction projects. Sometimes we got so dirty that our mothers swore they didn't recognize us.

During my sixth year, I received two wonderful gifts from my parents, a toy street packer and a road grader. These were quickly put to use building a road network in my backyard. Woody and I built a small town with roads crisscrossing the village in all directions. Once we had the roads in place, we used shoeboxes to make houses, tree branches to make telephone poles, and Popsicle sticks as signposts. An entire summer was spent building, rebuilding, and repairing our creation.

One hot afternoon, with our project in full development, we ran out of nails. There were no more in the garage; my father had given us all he could spare; and the Nances needed what they had. What to do? At this crucial hour, as moms are wont to do, Woody's mother called him home for nap; so I was left to my own resources to find the needed nails. While fretting over the problem,

I remembered seeing some rusty nails on the roof of the doghouse in the Asbury's backyard. My first thought was to ask the Asbury sister who taught music at home each day if I could have the nails, but I rationalized that by deciding that I did not want to bother her over such a small matter. *Surely*, I thought, *they don't care about some rusty nails. I'll just take them.* I entered Woody's backyard, crossed it stealthily so as not to be seen, and arrived at the fence separating the Chastain's yard from the Asbury's. The doghouse was almost touching the fence, so I reached over the fence, grabbed the nails, and beat a hasty retreat. The thrill of having those nails in my hand was exhilarating, to say the least, and every step to escape was even more exciting. In a moment of time, all of my Sunday school training, my grandmother's lectures, and my parents' guidance gave way to covetous desire and the thrill of getting away with petty larceny.

Back in my yard, I surveyed my treasure, nine rusty nails, which were bent and weakened by corrosion. Try as I might, I could get no use out of those nails and finally threw them on the ground.

Mother called me to supper, and I temporarily forgot my crime as I chewed on pork chops, sweet potatoes, and collard greens.

Things went fine until I went to bed at about eight o'clock. In my mind's eye, I relived the afternoon: the desire for the nails, the prelude to the crime, and the theft of the nails. Particularly vivid was the extraordinary feeling of exhilaration that accompanied the deed. Sleep would not come, and no matter what I tried, I just couldn't rest. One feeling had taken over, the feeling of guilt coupled with shame. My grandmother's face passed before me, a sharp finger poked my ribs, and her words thundered in my ears: "Hell was made for those who steal and lie." I hadn't lied yet, but I certainly had stolen. "Thou shalt not steal" came to me from the Ten Commandments I had learned in Sunday school. Tears welled up in my eyes as the sense of betrayal grew ever larger in my heart. Lying there in the dark, I thought about getting rid of the nails and saying nothing. After all, who would know I got them, or who would ever notice they were gone, nine rusty nails? But nothing eased my conscience, no matter what I concocted. Thinking it to be very late, I got up quietly to go to the bathroom; but as I entered the hall, I noticed a light on in the living room. Frozen in place for what seemed a very long time, I finally turned and ran quickly to the light.

"Son, what's the matter?" I heard my father say. "Why are you crying?"

"I . . . I stole some nails," I managed through my tears.

"You did what?"

"I took some nails that didn't belong to me."

"Where did you get them?" my father spoke firmly, but gently.

"I got them off the doghouse in the Asbury's yard. They were rusted and no good, so I took 'um."

My father took me in his arms and sat me on his lap. "What are we going to do about this?" I remained silent, hoping that we would—I don't know what I hoped. "You, young man," my father's voice had become assertive, "are going to return those nails to the Asburys tomorrow morning." I sat silent and ashamed.

"Why did you tell me about the nails, son? I might never have known."

"Grandmother taught me that I would go to hell if I lied or stole, and I don't want to go to hell and burn forever."

"Son, there is a much more important reason to be honest than a fear of hell. God loves us and has given us laws to govern our lives so that we won't hurt each other by lying or stealing. 'Thou shalt not steal' is God's way of telling us to respect the property of others. Tomorrow morning, first thing, take back the nails and tell the Asburys what you did."

"Will you go with me?"

"No! You were able to steal them on your own, so you'll have to return them on your own."

"But I don't have all the nails," I blurted out.

"Return what you have and ask the Asburys what you should do to repay them."

I did not sleep, fearing the Asbury's response. So as soon as I heard my parents in the kitchen the next morning, I went in and sat with my back to the warm oven of the oil stove as my mother fixed breakfast. Nothing was said as my father ate his eggs and toast, but as he got up to leave for work, he knelt down and gave me a hug. "I love you, son. I'll see you this afternoon."

"Can I go down and take the nails back as you go to work?"

"No. It's too early. You'll have to wait until about eight o'clock, then walk down and return the nails. Don't just leave them on the porch. Do you hear me?"

"Yes, sir."

"Speak to the Asburys and tell them exactly what you did. Do you understand?"

"Yes, sir."

I got up and went to my bedroom to await my doom. Time seemed to crawl by like the week before Christmas. My mother finally called me with the news it was time to go. I went out the back door to pick up the nails I had left in the yard. Gathering up what I could find, I turned toward Meadow Street and walked toward the Asbury's house. I knocked on the door, and when it opened, I said, "Good morning. I stole some nails off the doghouse." Tears were running down my cheeks.

"You did what?" Miss Asbury asked as she took the nails from my hand.

"I stole them from the doghouse."

"Why did you do that?" she asked. "You only had to ask, and we would have given them to you."

I stood crying and ashamed, unable to respond.

"Dickie, you're a much better boy than this."

"All the nails are not there. I broke the others."

"That doesn't matter. What matters is that you chose to steal. Have you learned anything?"

"Yes, ma'am," I said and turned for home.

When I entered the back door, my mother did not speak, and I went to my room and went back to bed. I slept past noon.

My father came home around six o'clock and walked back to my room where I had remained all day.

"Did you return the nails?" he asked.

"Yes, sir."

"How were you treated?"

"OK," I responded quietly.

"What's the matter?" he asked.

"I feel bad. I'm ashamed."

"Do I have to be concerned about such behavior in the future?"

"No, sir. Never! I don't want to feel this way again!"

"Good." And with that he took me in his arms and hugged me.

Neither my father nor the Asburys ever spoke of the matter again. They understood that further reminders were unnecessary. About two weeks later, Miss Asbury, the banker, asked me to take some money to Hollingsworth grocery for her and pick up an order. I ran the errand and returned quickly with the order and her change. She thanked me, handed me a nickel, and smiled. I skipped, hopped, and danced all the way home.

A June Apocalypse

I got up that late-June morning with no thought of a radical life change, but then, life-altering events are never truly anticipated. Nothing seemed out of place or different as I slipped on my loose-fitting white shirt and worn, but clean, blue jeans. Yawning freely, I sat on the edge of my bed and reached for the socks on the floor beside my Joe Lapchick tennis shoes (Michael Jordan hadn't yet been born). My mother would've had a fit if she had seen me putting on yesterday's socks, for she insisted on clean socks and underwear in case of an accident. But she wasn't in the room, and I had important things to do that didn't allow searching for clean socks. Eight dollars and some change lay on the nightstand beside my bed. Counting it carefully, I slipped the money into my pocket.

Looking around the room, I inventoried my chemistry lab with all its glassware and chemicals and surveyed my model-building bench, which stood empty and ready, waiting on my next project. My room was small with only one window that looked out over the front lawn, and directly opposite the window was a closet with sliding doors. There were few clothes in it, for chemistry and model-building equipment grabbed most of the space. Where were the clothes? On the floor, in a small chest between my lab and model-building tables, and on a chair. My parents avoided my room as if I or it had the plague. Frankly, I liked my room, although I needed more space to do experiments and to hang my models.

Standing up, I took one more look around the room, opened the door, and walked left down the hall and right into the kitchen. There seated at the table were my parents and two sisters. My father looked up with a smile and asked me about the day's activities. I said that I was going downtown to Bicycle Sales and Service.

"Can't wait to spend the money you've been earning? Burning a hole in your pocket?" asked my dad. "What is it this time? More chemicals or another airplane? You know, I ought to make you pay me for those new pants you ruined with acid." (I had spilled sulfuric acid on my pants and hid them in my closet. When Dad found them and picked them up, the left leg fell off.)

"Dad, you know I've done extra chores to pay you back, and besides, I've been saving my money to buy a Piper Tri-Pacer plane kit made by Berkeley Models. I have enough to get it and some necessary supplies. That's where I'm going this morning."

My mother interjected that the yard needed mowing and asked, "And just when do you intend to get that done?"

"Mom, I'll mow the yard this afternoon when I get back from town."

"See that you do," she said with a bit of an edge to her voice, for she knew that I would like to start the new model as soon as I returned.

One of my sisters entered the exchange with an unwanted observation, "You need to clean your room before you do anything. Don't you think so, Mom?"

"You mind your own business and eat your breakfast, young lady," said my mom. "But your sister is right about that room of yours. It seems to be leaking into the hall from time to time, don't you think?"

Before I could mount a defense, my father said, "Son, when you get back today, you have two chores—clean your room and mow the yard." He spoke with an I-mean-what-I'm-saying tone. I didn't respond. It wasn't necessary, and Dad knew it.

Dad finished breakfast and left for work. I enjoyed my eggs, bacon, and toast, though a bit too quickly for my mother, excused myself, and left the table.

At this point I knew that I had to escape the house as quickly as possible or my trip downtown would be delayed by still other chores that seem to lurk in every parent's head. So I left the house and walked briskly to get out of range of my mother's voice. I made it! The only problem was that it was just after seven o'clock, and Bicycle Sales didn't open until nine.

The month of June was ending with a heat wave, making the thought of a long stay downtown out of the question; so I walked up Ward Street and then left on English Street to a local grocery store. I enjoyed going to the store because liked the owner, Mr. Reed. He was a round little man of about five feet eight inches, a round face, reddish cheeks, and slicked-back black hair that was always covered by a butcher's hat. The only time he was without an apron was when he came to work and when he left. Bright, lively eyes peered through rimless glasses.

Those eyes drew you into his world and—coupled with a quick wit, sharp tongue, and ballet-like movements—made engaging Reed both a joy and a trial.

I entered the store and heard Reed ask, "You want to deliver groceries today? My dray boy didn't show up, heat I guess, so I got no help."

"Sorry, Mr. Reed, but I'm going downtown. I'll be here to work on Saturday as always."

"Make some good money if you'll work today. The bike is right outside, and Mrs. Harper is waiting on a delivery. If you don't deliver her groceries, I'll have to close the store and use the truck. What do you say?" Reed's eyes twinkled with mischievous delight. "I'll pay good."

I looked at the clock on the post behind the cash register and decided that I had time to make one delivery. "All right, I'll make this one delivery to Mrs. Harper." (She always gave a tip for prompt delivery.) "Is the order ready?"

"Yep, I'll help you load it," said Reed, with what I thought to be a note of real appreciation.

"But what'll you do about the rest of this morning's orders?" I asked.

"Don't worry. I'll get James (Reed's son) to come to the store and make the rest. It's just that Mrs. Harper needs this order right away to prepare lunch for her boarders."

Getting on the bike with a larger than expected box of groceries in the front basket wasn't easy to say the least, but Reed held the bike until I got some semblance of control. I looked down English Street to Ward and the steep hill that I had to negotiate. *Some way to avoid the heat,* I thought, and began pedaling. Reaching Ward Street, I started up the hill with real gusto, but I could only make it to the railroad overpass, which was about halfway up the hill. The load was just too much, so I got off the bike and walked it to the top. After that, the going was easier, and I arrived at Mrs. Harper's in fairly reasonable time. She was pleased to see her groceries and gave me a quarter. Going back was a breeze, as most of the trip was downhill. I parked the bike and went in the store. Reed, who was always as good as his word, reached into his pocket and gave me another quarter. By today's standards that's not much, but in 1953 it was a nice piece of change. I deposited the money safely in my jeans and went back to the soda cooler. I didn't want to spend a nickel, but I was hot and sweaty. Reaching into the ice water of the cooler, I pulled out a twelve-ounce Pepsi, opened it, and gulped it down. Walking back up front, I checked the clock again and left the store for the bus stop on English.

Reed yelled a "thanks" from the back of the store as I was leaving and reminded me that I was working Saturday. "Don't forget," he said. "I'll have a lot for you to do, and don't be late."

The bus was on time, and there were plenty of seats at that hour of the day, for the early workers had long ago gone to their jobs. I sat next to a window and watched lazily the passing homes and businesses that filled the landscape into West End and into downtown High Point. My thoughts were narrowly focused on that Piper Tri-Pacer.

I first saw and held that model in Thomasville at the radio-control flying field. One of the pilots made a beautiful side-hill landing about two hundred yards from where he was standing. He turned to me and asked if I would retrieve it for him. I ran all the way. The Tri-Pacer was covered with green silk and was beautifully constructed. So taken by the model, I stood studying it for several minutes. It was the biggest and heaviest model I'd ever seen, and I determined right then and there to build my own. It was easier thought than done, for the kit was over six dollars. I had to deliver a lot of groceries and mow several yards before I had enough. Finally, I was on my way to fulfill my dream.

The bus pulled up at S. Robinowitz Clothiers in the center of town at about 8:50 AM. I jumped off the bus and ran quickly down Main Street, arriving at Bicycle Sales just as the store opened. The Tri-Pacer had been sold. My heart sank, and I left the store dejected. Looking down Willowbrook Street that entered Main across from Bicycle Sales, I saw Dick Culler's Department Store. They had a few models, but I doubted that they would have the Tri-Pacer. What the heck, I'll walk down the block and see.

Upon entering the store, I climbed the steps to the second floor where the hobby shop was located. Kenny Bells was behind the counter. I liked Mr. Bells because he was always good to the children who came into his area. I ran up to the counter and breathlessly asked for the Berkeley Tri-Pacer, expecting no success. He smiled and pulled out the kit from beneath the counter. I couldn't believe it. I ran my fingers over the box gently as if expecting it to break. "Can I open it?" I asked. Then I quickly corrected my question, "May I open it?" remembering Mrs. Thayer's English class.

"Yes, you may," laughed Kenny, "but don't remove the box from the counter."

"I won't," I said, opening the box.

After carefully looking over the kit and studying the plans, I placed $6.50 on the counter. Kenny taped the box closed and placed it in a brown bag. I took it gently but firmly into my possession and turned to leave, in the excitement almost forgetting the building supplies. I turned back, finished my purchase, and left with a joy I hadn't experienced, perhaps ever. Maybe it was the satisfaction I felt from having earned the money to purchase the kit, but whatever the case, I was floating on air as I left the store.

Holding my precious cargo as if carrying a dozen eggs, I walked to Main Street and to the bus stop in the center of town, arriving some forty-five minutes before the bus was due. With time to kill, I walked down Main to Woolworth's Department Store to get a soda.

Woolworth's food counter was just inside the entrance to the left. I approached the counter, but accidentally went to the *wrong* end, the end for *colored people* as they were called in those days. I was told in no uncertain terms that if I wanted to be served, I would have to move to the *whites only* section. I moved and got my Coke. At eleven years old, I knew about segregation, but accepted it as the way things were at the time: white and black water fountains, bathrooms, restaurant, and bus seats, not to mention *Colored Town* and separate schools.

As I stood at the counter, I remembered a trip with my father to the black community off Kivett Drive. He had to pick up the family's laundry from Flossie, our washwoman, and took me along. I was much younger, but I remembered how different that area of town was from our own: dirt streets, few streetlights, run-down houses, poor sewage control, and a putrid smell, which I remembered for a long time. The washwoman's house was dilapidated and dirty on the outside, but clean and tidy on the inside. Clearly, she did as much a she could with what she could afford. I could see through the walls and floors, and I cried as we left to return home. Perhaps the memory was too painful to remember, for it had faded away until that moment at the Woolworth counter.

Leaving Woolworth's, I turned right and walked back up Main to the bus stop. The English Street bus was waiting. I got on and sat in the *white section* across from the entrance toward the rear. There was a broad white line at the back of the bus that divided the *white* and *colored* sections of the bus. Not until that day had the line stood out to me so severely. Nor had I noticed how few seats were available to the black community. In fact, the seats in the *black section* were already filled: there was standing room only.

As I waited anxiously to get my model home, I watched an elderly black lady approach the bus. She had gray hair, which matched the tired look on her face. She grabbed the handrail and made her way slowly up the steps. Her attire was that of a domestic worker—a blue dress and crumpled white apron. In her other hand was a brown bag which I thought, because of a small grease stain, contained her lunch. Her shoes were too large and run-down so that she walked on the sides of her shoes. She made a sliding sound as she shuffled to the back of the bus.

She stopped as she reached the white line. Looking for a seat, she found none. No one moved to offer her a place, even though she was a tired elderly woman. She turned around and stood behind the line, but tiredness apparently overcame her, and she crossed the white line and sat down in the *whites-only section.* She sat in a seat directly in front of the white line. No one spoke or moved as tenseness moved like a shadow over the black riders.

I turned toward the front of the bus and looked into the large rectangular mirror used by the driver. All that I saw were his eyes staring back. They narrowed and hardened.

"Get the hell behind that line! Do you hear me! Move!" The driver's voice was filled with contempt. His words were cold with the white heat of hate.

She didn't move. I think she was just too tired.

"Get the hell behind that line. If you don't, I won't move this bus, and I'll get a cop."

One of the black men got up and offered her his seat. He helped her up and assisted her to relocate. Tears streamed down her cheeks, but she never said a word. And what's worse neither did anyone else, including me.

"No respect for anybody!" continued the driver. "Ought to send all of 'um back to where they came from." With that, the driver closed the doors and started on his route.

I was ashamed, frightened, and angry. No one came to that lady's defense. As I looked at her face, I felt an undefined anguish that the world of the South where I lived was an unknown territory to me, at least it had been. Nothing would ever be the same for me again. Racism was a fact in my world, either as active participation or passive acceptance. Now, for the first time for me, it had eyes, a face, and a voice; and the victim had a face—a gentle, kind elderly face. A human being solely on the basis of color had been devalued, humiliated, and degraded in front of a busload of white people, and no one had objected, including me. Fear had paralyzed me in the land of adults, but why hadn't the grown-ups challenged the driver? They seemed to receive his behavior as perfectly acceptable, for they soon struck up conversations with him as if nothing extraordinary had happened. Laughing and joking, they didn't seem to care that someone's mother or grandmother had been viciously attacked. The truth is they would care more for an abused dog than for this African American lady.

The day had started with one world and ended with another: I had experienced a personal apocalypse.

The joy of buying a Piper Tri-Pacer model kit had been short-lived: it seemed completely unimportant now. I looked down at the model on the seat, no longer anticipating building or flying it. I turned my head to catch a glimpse of the elderly lady and felt sick. She looked emotionless, defeated, and bone weary. I wondered how she could continue to live in this world that devalued her existence and denied her meaning, a world that I had been immersed into unexpectedly. I hoped that she had some other community that loved her.

When I arrived home that afternoon, I went straight to my room and placed the model on the workbench. Wearily, I sat down on my bed and looked around my room. Nothing appeared as it had just that morning. Everything seemed to have changed in terms of value and importance. More importantly, I had changed and would never return again to the carefree childhood I had enjoyed just a few hours before.

Years passed, and I became a Christian pastor. The move to end Jim Crow segregation in the South and to bring equal treatment to black people had begun on many fronts. I often spoke to such matters and against racism, but almost always in safe situations, which cost me nothing—no risk, no pain, and no sacrifice. But nagging at my conscience was that incident on the bus; and a question disturbed my thoughts—would I stand up for that elderly African American lady now that I was grown up, or would I slink away in cowardice and defeat? I was good at challenging racism when it was safe to do so, but what if it demanded a price such as my life or hurt to my family? The answer was not long in coming.

I was serving a church near Hickory, North Carolina, an area going through the throes of court-ordered desegregation that required school redistricting and the busing of children. Local meetings almost turned into brawls, churches were divided, and the KKK was feeding the hate and disorder. My church too was divided about the matter with cliques forming for and against.

Late one Friday evening in the early fall, I received a call at the parsonage. A member of the church phoned to tell me that about half the congregation was attending a Klan rally on Highway 18 near Morganton and that they were Klan sympathizers, if not active members. At first, I couldn't believe the report, so Saturday morning I began to check the story. It was, unfortunately, all true.

I knew in my heart that this matter had to be addressed from the pulpit on Sunday, but the sermon had already been prepared. *Well,* I thought, *I can't change subjects at this point. Perhaps a soft easy approach was called for. Best not to say anything about the matter; after all, I could lose my job, and*

I had a wife and two very young children. And what about violence at the hands of the Klan? Could I expose my family to that?

As I sat in my office rationalizing my planned inaction, I suddenly found myself back on the bus and heard once more the vulgar vituperations of the driver, saw the face of the elderly lady, and felt the pain of my inaction. Working until late in the night, I prepared a new sermon that met racism with the firmness it required. Morning came and with it, fears—fear of being fired, fear of church turmoil, fear for my popularity, and fear for the well-being of my young family.

Sunday morning at eleven o'clock, I sat on the dais with two sermons in my Bible. One said nothing about the problems facing our community and the church; the other sermon met the problems head-on. Time seemed to slow to a walk, a sort of slow motion developed in my perception. Finally, the time to preach rose up before me like a sentencing judge.

I stood before the congregation with both sermons before me. They seemed to stare back at me with a silent challenge. My eyes slowly scanned the congregation for help, but none came. Suddenly as if out of body, I began speaking against racism, the Klan, and hate. After so many intervening years, I had found the voice to speak that I had lost on the bus when a little old lady needed a champion. That event I can never change, but I had remembered and acted.

So, that makes me a hero for speaking, right? Wrong! All I was that Sunday morning was a frightened sinner saved by the grace of the Holy Spirit, a broken man who had in his heart the memory of an African American lady who would never completely leave his thoughts.

The Last Breath

The entrance to the hospital glowed with a surreal mix of bright hospital lights and the inviting colors of Christmas lights. James stopped to take in the scene that seemed to mix sickness and death with the hope of the season. *But,* he thought, *isn't that exactly what is happening to me, and on Christmas Eve? I'm here to visit my dying father.* James stopped at the reception desk to get his father's room number and a visitor's pass. Slowly, hesitantly, he moved toward the elevators. After an agonizing wait, the elevator doors opened. For a moment James almost turned to leave, but swallowing hard, he entered and pushed the button for the third floor. With upward movement came the thought that he hadn't seen his father for about ten years; and as they both lived in the same small town, it had been difficult to avoid him. The elevator came to a stop, and James steeled himself for the meeting with a man he didn't like and prepared himself for the opening of old wounds, mostly his.

Standing at the foot of his father's bed, James found looking at his father difficult. *Could this be the vigorous man I have known all my life, the man who never let illness stop him? Once he even went to work with pneumonia,* James remembered, *and on another occasion with a partially collapsed lung. Now his hair is cotton white, and he's skin and bones. And that prominent jaw that I admired so much has drooped like the skin under a pelican's beak.* His observations were intensified by the dim lighting, the blinking lights of several life-support devices, and the cannula feeding oxygen into his father's nose. James felt sick and frightened.

"James, is that you? I can't see without my glasses," his father said with a whisper. "Why have you waited until now to come? Don't you care that I am dying? Oh, what's the use, you're a ne'er-do-well son," James's father began choking and coughing, shaking the bed violently, unable to finish his diatribe.

Yeah, that's my father all right, thought James. *He'll criticize me until he draws his last breath. What am I doing here? He never loved me.*

"James, James, is that you?" gasped his father.

"I'm right here," said James. *I don't know why. You don't really care whether I am or not,* he thought, bile welling up his throat.

"Come around here and hand me my glasses," wheezed his father.

"Where are they?"

"Where else would they be, but in the drawer. Why don't you think for once?"

"Here are your glasses. Look, I'm apparently upsetting you by my presence, so why don't I leave and come back later?" responded James, turning toward the door.

"Where are you going? Come back here right now," said his father.

"Who do you think you're talking to? The time is long past when you could order me around," shot back James with undisguised bitterness.

"I'm dying and you talk to me like that. You've always been ungrateful. You . . . you . . . ," James's father began heaving frightfully, unable to finish.

"This is absurd. I'm leaving. I've had enough of your verbal abuse, years and years of it." The door banged loudly behind James as he left.

His father raised himself up as far as he could to call his son back, but the emphysema was too far advanced to continue such effort. He fell heavily on the bed, gasping for air.

James slipped into his coat and walked slowly down the corridor. His mind was an arid desert of memories, memories of his father, memories that pricked like a cactus. Each one cut him, opening old sores and making new ones. He was so deep in thought that he didn't hear his name being called.

Suddenly, James felt a hand on his shoulder and heard a voice, "James, James, it's your pastor. Didn't you hear me?"

"No, Pastor, I'm sorry, I didn't," mumbled James.

"I was on my way to see your dad when I saw you leaving. You look like you're in a fog. Has your dad's condition worsened?"

"No, nothing like that! Dad is about the same, in more ways than one."

"What do you mean, James? Is there something I can help with?" asked the pastor.

"No, I don't think so. Just go and see my father. Perhaps I'll see you later at the midnight service."

"James, if there is anything you'd like to talk about, I'm willing to take all the time you need."

"I've got to go, Pastor."

"If I can help, just give me a call," responded Pastor Michaels.

James turned quickly away and headed for the elevators. He had to get outside for some fresh air. James found it difficult to breathe: his chest was constricted by emotion. The elevator ride seemed endless, and the tightness of his chest seemed to be collapsing his lungs. When he finally reached the lobby, he bolted for the door like a scuba diver racing toward the surface for oxygen. Standing on the hospital steps, he began to convulse with powerful sobs, crying uncontrollably. How long he stood there, he didn't know exactly, but long enough to remember the battles with his father.

His earliest childhood memory of his father was being chided for not running fast enough. James realized that there must have been times of joy, but he could only remember the flood of criticism that swept over him. The harder he tried, the more severe his father's judgments, like the one at his high school graduation. James had been an excellent student and had been named salutatorian of the graduating class, winning a scholarship to Duke University because of his many academic and social achievements. But on the day of graduation, his father met him after the exercises with the remark: "If you only you had worked a little harder, you could have been valedictorian. I'm sure that girl's father is really proud of her. Oh well, maybe you'll do better in college." James was shattered by his father's lack of pride in him, and the pain was exacerbated by the presence of fathers and mothers who showered praise on children who had accomplished far less. And so it had gone throughout his life. *I hold a doctorate,* thought James, *but my father has never acknowledged my accomplishment. In fact, I don't remember his ever telling me that he loved me. Never! To the devil with him, I'm not going back to the hospital. Let him die alone. That's all my old man deserves.*

Later that evening, as James sat alone in his apartment reading, the doorman rang to say that he had a visitor.

"Who is it?" inquired James.

"He says he's Pastor Michaels from First Baptist Church."

"What the devil does he want, that insufferable busybody," James mumbled under his breath. "All right, send him up."

A short while later, the buzzer shattered the quiet of the living room. The pastor had arrived.

"What do you want, Pastor Michaels? I really don't want to talk," James's response was graceless, and he positioned his body so as to block the pastor's entrance.

"James, I visited with your father for some time, and I need to talk with you. I know it's late, but this is important."

"Come in, come in," urged James, without hiding his irritation. "What do you need to tell me that is so important? Has he up and died already?"

"No, James, he hasn't died, at least not physically," responded the pastor, staring right into James's eyes.

"What is that supposed to mean? Leave your metaphysical mysteries for the pulpit," shot back James, responding to the pastor's stare with one of his own.

"Your father spoke to me tonight of his failure. He knows that he has hurt you deeply for most of your life."

"Oh great, the old man knows he has been a lousy father," responded a smirking James. "So tell me something I don't know."

"James, your father was raised in abuse and poverty by a father who blamed him for his wife's death. The fact that your father has been a productive human being is a tribute to his intense desire to rise above his beginnings," explained the pastor.

"Oh brother, so that excuses his emotional abuse of me. Wonderful! Look, Reverend, all I ever wanted was for my father to say he loved me. But he didn't. Do you understand what it means to grow up wondering if your father loves you? God knows I loved him and tried to please him," James was almost shouting.

"Did it ever occur to you that your father didn't know how to express his love for you?" the pastor asked deliberately.

"Let's see. He didn't know how to say 'I love you'? He didn't know how to put his arm around me and hug me? Pastor, you're not very convincing."

"James, you're implying that loving and accepting others is easy. Then why hasn't it been easy for you? I don't mean to hurt you, but your own life and bitterness is a testimony to your own failure," the pastor reached out and put his hand on James's shoulder.

James looked at the pastor with the shock of a man who has been knocked unconscious, but just hasn't fallen yet. He just stood speechless with tears trickling down his face.

When James finally found his voice, he said, "What are you trying to do to me?"

"I'm not trying to do something *to* you, but *for* you. Your father's life is chained by links forged from childhood to the present, links made of his father's blame, criticism, and lack of love. And now your own life is being wrapped with the same chain, forged of similar experiences. You must break that chain if you are to be free." The pastor now had both hands on James's shoulders.

"You're asking me to take responsibility for my father's failures," said James defensively, knowing the truth before he spoke.

"James, you know better than that. I am asking you to take responsibility for your own life."

"Where do I begin?"

"Begin by visiting your father and telling him how you feel. Let him know your pain and your need. If he is too ill to be told, just tell him that you love him. Tell him, James."

James found himself heading for the hospital. As he walked along, he thought of the painful relationship with his father and found it difficult to want to reach out to him, even at death. Understanding his father wasn't hard—forgiving him was.

James entered the room and went directly to the head of the bed and took his father's hand, which gripped back with trembling effort. James struggled to speak, but could not find the words. Finally, leaning close to his father, he hoarsely said, "I love you, Dad. Dad, I love you."

The old man tried to speak, but nothing came, nothing but a last breath. The struggle was over: a life had ended.

James stood silently by the bed. The words *I love you* were never offered to him, never shared. *What we could have been to each other over the years. What we could have shared*, thought James. *It's too late for that now. How can two people live together . . . how, for God's sake, can a father and a son be so far apart? What a waste! What an awful waste!* His thoughts exploded into the room as a monosyllabic groan.

As James was leaving the room, the pastor was coming down the corridor. "James, how is your father? Were you able to speak with him?"

"Pastor, he's dead. He died just a few minutes ago. I told him that I loved him, but he was unable to speak. I never heard my father tell me that he loved me."

"I'm sorry, James, that your father died before telling you that he loved you, but I assure you that he did with all his heart. I suppose that doesn't help much, but it is the truth. He told me how much he loved and respected you, the only member of his family to graduate from college. What a shame that he couldn't tell *you!*"

"Pastor, can we go to a quiet waiting area and talk for a few minutes. I know that you have Christmas Eve services in a little while, but there is something I need to say."

"Certainly, James, let's go down to the solarium. It will probably be empty at this hour."

The two men sat quietly at first. In time, James began by returning to the conversation in his apartment earlier that evening. "Pastor, what you said to me a few hours ago struck home with a terrible force. You were right about my life. It has become a sinkhole of bitterness, lovelessness, and loneliness. I have driven my friends away and held at arm's length every acquaintance. My anger at my father has been turned against others. My God, how I hate the happiness of others! How ugly I have become. You know that I've been dating . . . I *was* dating Jill Lane from our church. I have forced her out of my life by the same ugliness that my own father offered to me. How can I break this chain and rebuild my life? I want to forgive my father and remember him with love in my heart."

"James, the boy I baptized years ago with faith on his lips and love in his heart is not dead, but wounded. Turn to your Lord and run into his arms, for he will receive you with all the joy of heaven. Your Father in heaven has loved you so much that his own Son came to earth on this night to save and redeem your life. In the very heart of God, you will learn to forgive your earthly father and love freely once more. Jesus didn't teach us that wrong is right or that what your father has done is acceptable. But Jesus teaches us the way of love and forgiveness, for only by this way can this world change and our lives have a new future. The very presence of the Kingdom of God is everywhere and anywhere that we give love and forgiveness in the name of Jesus. The real blessing of Christmas is the future promised by

Jesus and made possible by his love and forgiveness. A good place to begin anew is at the Christmas Eve service. Why don't you come?"

"Pastor, I'll join you there in a little while. I have something I want to do."

"All right, James, I'll see you there. Oh yes, if you're still interested, Jill and her family will be there. Should I have them save a place for you?"

"I don't know, Pastor. Jill may not want to see me. I've hurt her badly."

"Oh, you might be surprised, James." And with that the two men parted.

James walked back up the corridor to his father's room. He stood at the foot of the bed for a long time, looking at his father's body. After a prayer for forgiveness for himself and his dad, he said, "I love you, Dad." And with that, James took a long last breath in a painful past and turned toward the future.

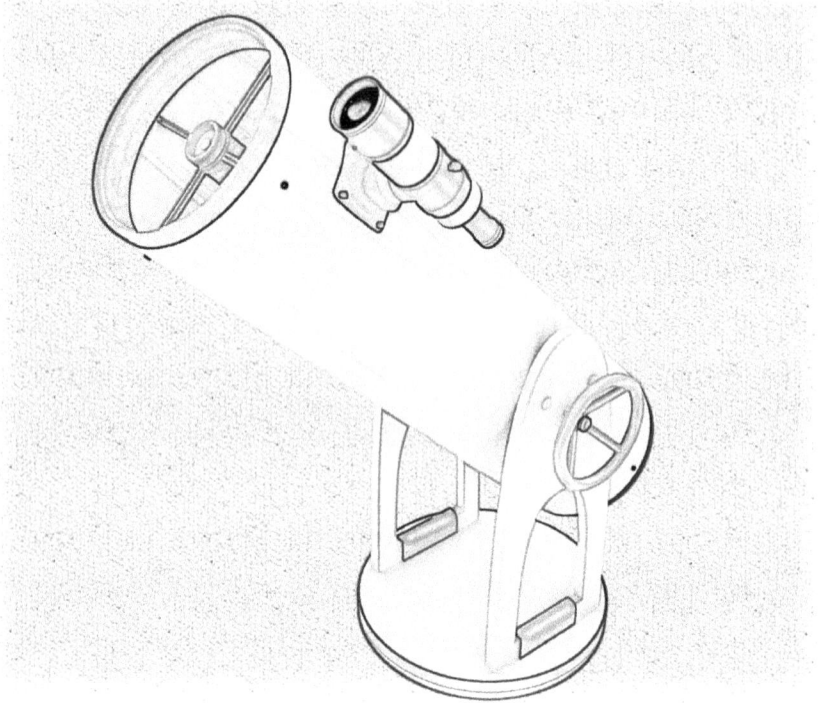

The Telescope

Mimi so loved Christmas that she had trouble sleeping during the week before. Oh, she would go to bed at her usual time of nine thirty, but visions of Christmas Day and glittering presents danced before her eyes, pushing sleep into the wee hours of the morning. And this Christmas just might be her best yet, making sleep the last resort of an overexcited and tired young girl. You see, Mimi had asked for one present and only one for several months: a ten-inch Dobsonian telescope.

Mimi's request for a telescope had initially not been received well by her parents, especially her father. Both parents wanted her to be like *all other girls* and ask for gifts such as makeup kits, clothes, CDs of the latest music, and other *appropriate* gifts for a near-teenager. Mimi's father was the worst in terms of attitude: "Mimi, I refuse to buy a boy's gift for my daughter. You should be interested in girl things."

"But, Dad, girls like astronomy too."

"Maybe so, but you're Daddy's little girl, and that's all there is to it."

Mimi's mom did try to mediate a bit, for she had always wanted a daughter she could dress up in the latest clothes and teach all the female things, but her attempts were somewhat weak at best. Her mother had died when she was a child, so she never had the opportunity to share life with a mom. And now that she had a daughter of her own, things were not as she had dreamed.

Mimi *was* different. She was a dedicated student, reader, and a budding naturalist. Her face was slightly oval with large brown eyes, a slightly long nose, and a thin mouth that had a cute little twist when she smiled. Mimi was tall for her age and skinny. She pulled her hair back in a careless ponytail and maintained it with a rubber band, but even her best efforts could not keep strands of hair from falling onto the sides of her face and into her eyes, which she blew out of the way at crucial moments. Glasses were her necessary companion, and she did not dress in keeping with the latest style. Rather, her wardrobe was determined by what was practical for catching salamanders, hunting for snakes, and walking through the park with her bird-watching binoculars. In an *image-is-everything* world, Mimi had the wrong one. Frankly, she didn't much care, although some of the treatment by her peers was dismissive and very painful. What hurt her the most, however, was that her parents sometimes looked at her the way her classmates did, as if she was not quite what they wanted. At least that's what she thought. This was most acutely felt when she returned from one of her nature excursions and was met by her mother's cry of horror at the sight of her dirt-covered daughter, hair a mess, clothes askew, and tick infested.

Astronomy? Where did that interest come from? After all, how many twelve-year-old girls ask for a ten-inch Dobsonian telescope for Christmas? Mimi had never given much thought to sky watching until her parents took her to the Moorehead Planetarium in Chapel Hill, North Carolina, when Mimi was about ten years old. One look at the Zeiss projector, the magnificent night scenes projected onto the dome, and the fascinating photographs of the planets and Mimi was swept away into the heavens. The following Christmas she received, after a near act of Congress, a small refracting telescope with an altazimuth mount—a child's toy that didn't take long to outgrow. For two years she had been pleading for a larger scope, but her parents had ignored her requests in the hope that her interest would dwindle away and that parties and dances would bring her vision back to earth. After all, she's a girl and should be interested in *girl things*.

Two days before Christmas, the gifts were piling up around their Christmas tree. Mimi had added her gifts for her parents and was pleased that she had gotten them meaningful gifts. She always took great care to discover what they wanted and saved her money to make the purchases. Everything she spent on Christmas was earned by doing odd jobs for the neighbors and babysitting the twins next door.

As she surveyed the presents under the tree, Mimi could find nothing that remotely met the size requirements for a ten-inch telescope, nothing at all. Oh, there were gifts with her name on them, but nothing that was four feet long and weighed about fifty pounds, not to mention the base on which the tube was supported. She began to resign herself to the fact that if she wanted a new telescope, she would have to earn the money and buy it herself. But resignation didn't ease the pain of having her deepest desire ignored by her parents.

Her eyes moved up from the gifts to the tree that her parents and she had decorated shortly after Thanksgiving, which was a family custom. The balsam fir was particularly beautiful, shaped perfectly and thick with branches. Many of the ornaments were handmade family heirlooms, some were her creations, and others were specially selected to remind the family of important events that they shared. There was one with a picture of her, front teeth missing, centrally displayed on the tree. *Now, that's embarrassing,* she thought, not knowing exactly why she suddenly disliked the picture. How to light the tree had caused a good-natured family debate. *Should the tree have multicolored lights, all one color, lights that flashed on and off, or bubble lights?* After no small amount of back-and-forth, they agreed on white lights, small star lights. The glow of the tree warmed her heart and temporarily dulled her growing disappointment.

Christmas Eve came, and preparations for Christmas dinner were at a frantic pace. Mimi and her mother spent the entire Saturday making cookies and cakes, mixing salads and stuffing, preparing bread, vegetables, and the twenty-five pound turkey that was needed to feed the large family gathering.

She had no chance to survey the gifts, forgetting everything but dinner preparations and going to church for the candlelight service.

Mimi loved that service more than any other during the church year, and she couldn't wait to see the sanctuary this year, for the congregation had purchased a large Moravian star to hang over the manger scene. As the family entered the church, Mimi caught her first glimpse of the star, and her heart jumped with joy at how beautiful it was. She was a Christian, having been baptized on the previous Easter Sunday morning. This Christmas Eve service was even more meaningful than usual. After it was over, she continued to sing "Silent Night" softly to herself all the way home.

Christmas Eve at home was special, because the family sat and talked at the fireplace while the Yule log burned brightly. As they drank mulled cider and ate Christmas goodies, Mimi and her parents shared their love for each other and laughed and joked about their lives and what tomorrow would bring. The previous Christmas Eve had not been pleasant, because Mimi had pouted at not getting a better telescope, feeling particularly hurt and misunderstood by her parents. But this year, she had made up her mind that no matter what happened, she would be thankful for her gifts, especially for her family and the goodness of God.

As Christmas Day was on Sunday, the family ate a quick, light breakfast and went to church. There was no time to open gifts. As soon as the service was over, the family rushed home to get ready for their guests. Fourteen family members gathered around the dining room table and shared a joyous meal with no little amount of Christmas high jinks. This was followed by exchanging gifts in the living room, singing carols, enjoying dessert, and just being with each other.

When lethargy began to set in, the room became quiet and the people mellow. The silence was broken when Mimi's father and mother began telling the family how proud they were of their daughter and her achievements: "The science teacher told us that Mimi is an exceptional math and science student with a great future," said her dad, smiling and hugging her.

"She won the school science fair last fall and is helping to prepare an exhibit for the spring, and she didn't even tell us," added her mom.

"I don't know where she gets it," observed her grandfather. "After all, Victoria, you wouldn't even put a worm on your hook when I took you fishing," speaking to Mimi's mom. Victoria just blushed and chuckled. "I hear that Mimi hunts snakes and creepy crawlers," continued her granddad. "Mimi, I'll have to take you fishing this spring and see if you can bait your own hook."

"Just show me the worms, Granddaddy," Mimi responded with a big grin.

Mimi's mom did add that she wished Mimi would put on something frilly now and then, but she'd have to leave that to her daughter.

Needless to say, Mimi was overcome with what she was hearing and settled easily into the warm acceptance of her family. She had received the best present she could ever have received.

After the kidding and banter ended, the family slowly said their holiday wishes and departed. The sun had set, and darkness had gathered around the warm and happy home.

"We haven't opened our presents yet. What's the holdup?" asked Mimi's dad.

"What's the holdup?" repeated Victoria. "We've had a very busy day. That's the holdup, not to mention that our messy kitchen awaits."

Groans issued forth from the family, but attention was centered on their gifts. Mimi's father handed the first gift to Victoria and then one to Mimi. This went on with hugs and kisses until all the presents had been opened. There was no telescope. Mimi was very disappointed, but did not let it show.

After they stuffed torn paper and crumpled ribbons into a trash bag and repaired the damage done to the living room, they started toward the kitchen to do the dishes.

"Mimi, before we clean the kitchen, let's go out on the patio for a few minutes," suggested her dad. Her mom and dad took her by the hands and led her outside through the sliding door on the sun porch. "Now, shut your eyes, dear," said her mom. After turning on the patio light and carefully negotiating the steps, her dad told her to open her eyes. There before her stood the ten-inch Dobsonian that she so badly wanted.

"I read the book that came with the telescope, and it stated that I should allow the telescope to sit in the cold so that the mirror could adjust. So while you were helping your mother, I stealthily carried it outside to the dismay of my back. This thing weighs a ton!"

Mimi had tears in her eyes as she hugged her parents and tried to say *thanks*. She touched the telescope gently and then threw her arms around it as if she were greeting a long lost friend.

Suddenly, to her parents' surprise, she dashed into the house and raced to the telephone. After a brief conversation, she ran to her room and shut the door.

"What in the world is going on?" asked her father. "Doesn't she like the telescope?"

"Of course she does," responded her mother.

Both parents just stood staring at the door of their daughter's room and were completely baffled.

After what seemed an eternity, the door to Mimi's room opened and out stepped a twelve-year-old young lady. Her hair was down to her shoulders, she was wearing a new blouse and skirt, and she was carrying her jacket and boots.

At just that moment, the doorbell rang, and Mimi dashed to open it. As the door opened, Mimi's parents saw a young fellow, slightly taller than Mimi, the son of one of their neighbors.

"This is Tommy. He wants to be a scientist too. We're in the same classes at school. I invited him over to look through my new telescope. I know I should've asked, but I was so excited that I forgot. Is it all right?"

As Mimi and Tommy walked by, Mimi's parents looked at each other and laughed softly. They still had a lot to learn about their daughter.

Rahab

"What if he will not see me?" she whispered as she hurried through the winding streets of Jerusalem. "What if, what if . . . All I know is that I must reach him and ask him a question and give him a gift."

The dark serpentine streets through which Rahab fled were like the ways of her own life: twisted and tortured, littered by garbage, and reeking with ugly smells that could not be washed or perfumed away.

A door opened suddenly to her left, and a dark figure loomed in the doorway. Rahab choked back a scream. Nearly breaking into a run, she remembered the looming presence of her drunken father coming to her bed. He had hurt her again and again, and no one had protected her. Rahab stumbled and fell into an open sewer, but she kept the nard from spilling. She stood up and tried to clean her clothes, but it was no use.

Rahab glanced back and shuddered at the hulking shadow still framed in the door of his house. Once more, her past thrust into her present. Men had been solicited by her father to come and use her for money. She remembered no faces or names, or even what they did, only the smell of the sour wine on their breath. She started to retch, forced by her heaving to lean against the wall of a house. The nausea passed as a wave of anger swept over her fragile body, and she stood with her head against the wall and pounded at the mud bricks furiously with her left hand. She stopped only after she felt blood trickling down her arm. Rahab slid to the ground and lay in a fetal curve; she prayed to die.

As she lay at the base of the wall, Rahab began to remember her one and only meeting with Jesus. Elements of the meeting came and went—broken and confused—out of sequence. It was like wind swirling over a lake and creating conflicting ripples that cancel each other out. No, it was like a person walking away while talking to you: after a while you stop trying to listen. Wearily, she propped herself up and tried to clear her mind.

She met Jesus at a party thrown by one of her lovers, a wealthy publican. It was a bash thrown in honor of the Roman officials who supervised the collection of taxes. She and several other women had been invited to provide "entertainment," or so it was described by the host. Entertainment meant doing anything the Romans wanted. The pay was good.

Everything was going as expected until he entered. Jesus and three of his companions had been invited by the host, but never did he expect Jesus to come. Suddenly, in the midst of a rowdy, licentious gathering stood the rabbi and his disciples.

Rahab remembered approaching him, preparing to take his arm and escort him to his host, when one named Peter stepped between her and Jesus. "Women are not allowed to touch the rabbi, especially one of *your* kind," he declared contemptuously. She was pushed away roughly.

"Peter, let the woman pass," Jesus said, offering his arm to Rahab.

"But, Master, she's a-a-harlot," Peter rasped incredulously.

"Please lead me to my seat," Jesus said to Rahab without noting Peter's remark.

As she stepped forward to take Jesus' arm, Rahab watched his eyes. Rahab knew that his gaze would undress her and coldly appraise her for his pleasure. All men are the same, users and abusers. But Jesus looked into her eyes and smiled the most compassionate smile she had ever seen. For a moment, her knowledge of men was shaken. Then a wave of insecurity swept over her. Perhaps he didn't want her because her body did not excite him. *I'm not good enough for you, is that it?* she thought angrily. *Who are you to reject me, you uncomely holy man, you poverty-stricken teacher. Ha! You couldn't pay me enough to take your bed.* Rahab brought Jesus to his couch and smiled perfunctorily into his open face. His look was gentle and kind.

"What is your name?" asked Jesus.

"Rahab," she nearly spit the syllables out, imagining his rejection.

"Thank you," Jesus said as he reclined.

Rahab turned away. She had a job to do and plenty of opportunity to prove she was desirable. Her need for attention was soon met by one of the Roman officials, Octavian. He grabbed at her as she passed and pulled her to him. His breath was sour with wine. From time to time during her tussle with Octavian, Rahab tried to catch Jesus' eye. She wanted him to desire her. She wanted something.... But only once did Rahab see him look at her, and Jesus' expression was sad, yet compassionate, as if he understood her actions and their cause.

Now, as Rahab leaned against the clammy wall, she couldn't remember the whole story, but a part of it was very clear. A wayward son had received his inheritance and wasted it in riotous living. This son had finally stooped to living among swine. The part Rahab couldn't forget, even to perfect detail, was what happened when the son returned home in a wretched condition:

So he set off and went to his father. But while he was still far off, his father saw him and was filled with compassion; he ran and put his arms around him and kissed him. Then the son said to him, 'Father, I have sinned against heaven and before you; I am no longer worthy to be called your son.' But the father said to the slaves, 'Quickly, bring out the robe—the best one—put it on him; put a ring on his finger and sandals on his feet. And get a fatted calf and kill it, and let us eat and celebrate; for this son of mine was dead and is alive again; he was lost and is found!' And they began to celebrate.

When Jesus finished and turned to go that night, Rahab found her way to his side. Jesus turned and said to her, "Rahab, your true Father is in heaven, and the true Father loves you."

In the present darkness, Rahab struggled to her feet. *I must go to Jesus and ask him if what he said really applies to me,* she thought. *I must ask that question. I must.* She picked up her vial of nard and hurried down the street.

As she approached the house where Jesus was teaching, she ran headlong into two of her former patrons. "Hey, don't we know you? Sure, you're Rahab. Got anything for us? Come on, whore. Let's have some fun."

Rahab tried to flee from their attention, but they pursued her to the very door of the house where Jesus was. As she opened it to enter, one of the men grabbed her and forced her into his embrace.

"Come on, woman, let's go. Don't worry! I have money. I can pay." The door was open, and the room had grown quiet. Jesus had heard everything.

"Leave her alone," Jesus said sternly. "She deserves no such treatment."

"Who are you?" said one of the men.

"I am Jesus of Nazareth," said Jesus.

"So you're Jesus of Nazareth, are you? What do you care about this whore? Do you want her for yourself?" he growled with a sly grin.

"Yes, I want her, but not in the way you mean. I want to talk to her," said Jesus.

"Then have her, Rabbi." The man hurled the title as if it were a dagger. He shoved Rahab forward, and she fell at Jesus' feet.

She lay on the floor, smelling of the street—dirty, bloody, and humiliated.

The crowd in the room pulled back, not wanting to be contaminated by such a creature. Whispered comments and knowing looks raced around the room like a wind racing through a wheat field. Yet it was the crowd's own self-righteousness that was ready to be harvested.

"Rahab," Jesus spoke gently and openly, "why have you come?"

"Master, I have come to ask you a question, but now I'm sure I know the answer."

"What is your question?"

"Look at me. I'm exactly what those men outside said I am, a whore. But you know that, don't you?" She could not raise her eyes.

"Rahab, what is your question?" Jesus opened his hand to her to help her up.

The crowd gasped with horror that he had touched her.

"Rabbi, you told a story about a wasteful son who returned home and received his father's love. Do you remember the parable you told that night at the party?"

"Yes, Rahab, I remember."

Rahab was silent for an excruciating moment. "Is God like the father in that story?"

"Rahab, God loves all of his children far beyond what that parable can depict," said Jesus.

Rahab looked Jesus in the face. "Even a whore like me?" she said without flinching.

"God knows the sins of all God's children and loves them unsparingly."

"But I'm a woman, Lord, not a son."

"God loves you, and I also love you. Sin no more."

In response, Rahab opened her container of nard and anointed Jesus' feet. She wiped his feet dry with her hair.

"Rahab, I have a disciple, Mary Magdalene, who can help you. She will understand what you have suffered, and she will give you lodging." Jesus gave her the instructions that she needed. "Go, daughter of God."

As Rahab entered the dark streets again, she knew what she faced. Her past would not be put away easily. The word "whore" would follow her for some time. She would not forget the dark shadows approaching her bed, the smell of sour wine, the love for hire. But she knew beyond all of this that she was truly loved—that she was God's child. Rahab was filled with the hope that the new wine of the kingdom that opened before her would smell sweet.

Madeline

I don't know how many times I saw Madeline throw mud (clay) on her potter's wheel and begin the demanding task of producing a work of art, but each time seemed completely new and wondrous. As the wheel turned, an ugly wad of dirt was transformed into a vase, a plate, a cup, or any number of other creations.

Madeline's fingers and feet worked in a marvelous coordination so that just the right pressure on the clay was matched by just the right speed of the wheel. I once heard a professor friend describe how Joachim Jeremias went into a trance-like state as he did form-critical analysis of a Gospel passage. Suddenly the world was excluded as his mind moved over the ancient writings with faithful care.

Something similar happened as Madeline worked on the clay, for the act of turning was a spiritual event fed from deep in a soul attuned to God's profound love for his world. One of her favorite passages of scripture was Isaiah 64:8, "Yet, O Lord, you are our Father; we are the clay, and you are our potter; we are all the work of your hand." As Madeline bent over the wheel, she could imagine God's hands molding her life and the lives of her husband, her children and grandchildren—ultimately the lives of everyone in the world.

And when the turning went badly and the vessel under creation was marred, Madeline would remember out loud Jeremiah 18:1–4, "The word came to Jeremiah from the Lord: 'Come, go down to the potter's house, and there I will let you hear my words.' So I went down to the potter's house, and there he was working at his wheel. The vessel he was making of clay was spoiled in the potter's hand, and he reworked it into another vessel, as it seemed good to him." Then she would rework the seemingly hopeless mess on the wheel into a beautiful creation with no sign of error. Madeline's view of humanity was like that: *marred as we are, God can turn us into beautiful vessels filled with God's love and purpose.*

Madeline and I met and became friends when I moved to Valdese as a young pastor. I was in my late twenties and she in her early seventies. For several years she was my church secretary. During that time of close contact, I realized that her life had not been an easy one. Married to a potter meant, in those days, facing financial hardship, especially when a small income had to feed several hungry mouths. She, like other good parents, sought the best for her children. Her early mornings, late nights, and time over the potter's wheel were times of prayer for her family, friends, and neighbors. Early mistakes in her own life, as it should with all of us, reminded her of the need for love and grace, which she gave in abundance. The parable of the potter's wheel from Jeremiah was always with her as she looked at her own flaws, those of her family, her friends, and the pastor. No one was a throwaway, not one. No one would ever be beyond the net of her grace or the power of her love. She was at times like Santa Claus at Christmas, everywhere. When elderly friends needed transportation to doctors, grocery stores, and other necessary places, she was there for them, providing safe travel. When food was needed to help the sick, she could always be counted on to provide a dish, even if her own pantry was a little bare. Sick neighbors received cards and visits. Wayward acquaintances often were given a loving but pointed comment or two about faithfulness and courage. On one occasion, suffering from a severe and very painful case of phlebitis, she received a friend's call for help and hobbled around an entire afternoon giving assistance. Her sacrifice for others was without strings and never used to extract favors in return. The Great Potter had made her, and she was just being thankful by doing a little potter's work herself.

If you had passed her on the street, you probably would have taken no notice, for the living of seventy and more years had marked her face with folds of wrinkles born of life's cares, and the wrinkles fit perfectly with the heavy snow on the roof. Her clothing left a lot to be desired, for she took little notice of outward appearance in favor of an inner beauty that only God can provide. Seeing her on the street, you might have dismissed her as another frumpy old lady who was just too tired to take care of her appearance. Yet, if your eyes met hers, there just might be a dramatic change of attitude, for they were as bright as the lights that guide ships safely into harbor. Speak to her, and a marvelous wisdom flowed gently from a secret place molded by God's Spirit. Walk with her, and the world took on a newness that pointed to new creation. Sit with her, and a peace that passes all understanding was offered without thought or pretense. Eat at her table, and the communion of saints was not far away.

As I wrote above, I was a young pastor when I moved to Valdese. As the new pastor, Madeline took pity on me, my youth and inexperience. Filled with the hubris of ordination, I was no bargain as a minister. Frankly, I had little of the experience necessary to understand the needs of older members; and Linda and I were parents of two small children, which meant that we were struggling in about the same way as other young families. All in all, I felt at times, between bouts of ministerial arrogance, that I was as *ignorant as dirt*. When I was about to jump on a hobbyhorse and ride off in all directions at once spouting the language of Zion, Madeline would gently grab the reigns and help me get control of my petulance. At other times, she would gently prod me to make a visit to a disgruntled church member or to shut-in. She was well aware of what we pastors call the *gotcha* game. This is the game some members of the church play when they go to the hospital or become shut-in without informing the pastor. Then, when—out of ignorance—the pastor doesn't make a call, the hurt church member informs others of the pastor's failure. *GOTCHA!* Madeline often kept me out of trouble by informing me of unspoken needs in the church. She was, in fact, gently training me to be a pastor. The old potter was struggling mightily with the young stiff clay of the pastor.

Linda and Madeline helped bring my youthful enthusiasm under control and direct it toward a loving concern for others. Older pastors learn that the degrees, the call, and the ordination do not make a pastor. Only God's Holy Spirit, working through a good wife and someone like Madeline, can form an oversized ego into a shepherd of the church. So the days and years passed at Valdese with Madeline's prodding me in the right directions at the right times.

I can remember as if yesterday the morning that Madeline entered my office and informed me of her chronic back pain. She told me that she would be leaving early to visit the local chiropractor. What he saw on her x-ray caused him to send her to an internist who specialized in oncology. Madeline was diagnosed with cancer. The tumor was virulently aggressive and had spread from internal organs to her spine. On a snowy day, I road in an ambulance with her and members of her family to Charlotte for a second opinion and possible treatment options.

She was sent home to die. In her dying, she gave me spiritual life.

I was not prepared for Madeline to die, so I began visiting her and having long prayer sessions with her. Every time I went I declared my *faith* that God would work a miracle and spare her life. The congregation joined me in this determined effort of saving Madeline by having many prayer sessions and by doing much visiting to encourage her. When she tried to talk to me about her needs and death, I would hear none of it and talked over her attempts to face dying. The truth was that I was afraid of where Madeline was trying to take me, for I had lost my grandfather to cancer at age eleven and could not bear the loss of another person so close to me. All of this is not to suggest that we should not pray for the sick and dying. Certainly, we should. God does work miracles in our world all of the time, but we must leave that to God's ultimate will and ready ourselves to minister properly to the dying when that hour comes.

One afternoon I entered Madeline's bedroom for a visit and started the same approach I had been using for several weeks: denial, talking over Madeline's concerns, and using prayer as an early escape from the room when the situation became uncomfortable. Suddenly, mustering all of her energy, she interrupted me rather harshly.

"Stop this right now! Stop it!" she said.

Shocked, I could not respond, but stood, mouth open, looking at her.

"Stop running away. I'm dying." She continued, "And I need your help. I need for you to care about me and not yourself."

Choking back the bile in my throat, I tried to protest, but nothing coherent came out. The best I could do was to mutter a lame denial, and I wasn't sure what I was denying.

"Pastor," she went on, "there are things I need for you to do for me, so that I can die in peace. Will you help me?"

My face became hot, and tears welled up in my eyes. For what seemed a long time I couldn't speak; not a word would come. Finally, looking into her pleading eyes, I told her I would do anything she wanted.

"There are times when you came that I needed just your presence, and I just about screamed when you would start in about my not dying or quickly went to prayer to prevent my speaking. Pastor, come and just sit with me. Will you?"

"Yes, Madeline, just tell me what you need when I come, and I'll do it."

"Pastor, there are times when I want you to pray with me and read the scripture to me; but often I want to talk about my life, to sort out things. I want to talk about dying. There are many things I need to share with you and some things I need to settle with my family. You can run some interference for me, for they don't want to talk about these matters either. Do you understand?"

"Yes," I responded, feeling very uncomfortable about her comments. Frankly, I didn't want to go where she was taking me. I was afraid, very afraid.

From that day until the end of her life, I went to her to meet her needs. Sometimes, we were silent for the entire visit while I held her hand. On other occasions, I read the scriptures to her; and on others, I prayed with her for grace to meet the coming days and the end of her life. Many hours were spent listening to life concerns, family matters that needed settling, and what she wanted as part of her funeral service. Madeline's Christian faith was evident in all that she said and did and was guiding her down the road to life eternal.

For the first time, I truly internalized what it meant to be a pastor. Listening, I discovered, had not been a part of my ministry; for I thought I was expected to have all the answers. Madeline taught me the value of silence in the presence of another's words. Suddenly, it dawned on me that God's grace was sufficient to the needs of the hour, that Jesus is the Savior, not I, and that the love of Christ will lead us if we get out of the way.

During those visits, I learned how to pray. Oh, I was good at mouthing prayers, but poor at praying. Sitting beside this dying woman, I learned to pour out my heart to the Father, the Son, and to the Holy Spirit. My heart opened to the will of God and to God's love for his children. The Psalms and the rest of the Bible took on new meaning in the sanctuary of prayer. Instead of the Bible being a magic book read at times of need, it became a voice of God's correction and healing for every occasion of life.

With listening and prayers came tears, honest tears for another person and for myself. Instead of pastoral affectation, I learned of my own humanity, pain, and feelings for those around me. I became aware of the cost of loving and the decision that must be made to take the risk. Instead of playing a role, I learned at Madeline's bedside about the pastor as person and about being honest with my fellow human beings and the God who made me.

Madeline—in life and in death—had been my pastor, and for that I shall always be grateful.

The time came for Madeline to return to the God who made her. Her death was exceedingly hard and long. Courageous to the end, she died at Valdese General Hospital. Her funeral was simple, but it was a powerful expression of her faith and the hope that filled her soul. Spiritually, Madeline was as sturdy and beautiful as her pottery, and she was a wonderful potter who began work on the lump of clay that I am, leaving an unfinished vessel in the hands of God.

The Fool

"How dare he say that to me! To *me*! Does he think me a fool?"

"What are you talking about, David?" asked Jeremiah.

"That, that would-be rabbi, Jesus, told me to give away all that I have and follow him! Who does he think he is, God's Son?" David was almost shouting as he remembered the conversation.

"Hold on there," interjected Jeremiah. "I don't understand what you're talking about. Start from the beginning."

David stood silently for what seemed like a long time, his face caught in an ugly frown. But before he spoke, he forced his face back into its normally handsome expression.

"Jeremiah, I recently went to Capernaum on business. You remember. I took an order of drapery material to one of our customers. Well, on the way back, I came across a rather large crowd, just standing by the road listening to a teacher. My curiosity got the best of me, so I stopped to listen."

"What was he saying?" queried Jeremiah.

"It wasn't so much what he said, although that was remarkable, but how he said it. He spoke with an authority that even our greatest Scribes and Pharisees do not possess . . ." David's voice trailed off as he remembered Jesus' face and manner.

"Well, go on, man," urged the impatient Jeremiah, who was now thoroughly confused by David's mixed reactions. First there was his initial explosion of anger, but this was now followed by an extraordinary distraction.

"Jeremiah, I was so drawn to him that I pushed my way past the adults and children and found myself looking into his eyes. And do you know what?"

"No, what?" Jeremiah said, his voice unable to mask his growing irritation.

"I blurted out, 'Good teacher, what must I do to inherit eternal life?' Do you hear me, Jeremiah? What do you think of a man of my standing asking a poverty-stricken itinerant teacher about eternal life? Why, I've known the law from my childhood, and I—"

"Yes, I know how good you are. How could I ever forget?" Jeremiah said with a wry smile twisting his bearded face. "So what did he tell you?"

"This Jesus responded, 'Why do you call me good? No one is good but God alone. You know the commandments: You shall not commit adultery; you shall not murder; you shall not steal; you shall not bear false witness; honor your father and mother.' I certainly put him straight in a hurry," said David with what seemed a forced certainty.

"What did you tell him?" urged Jeremiah.

"I said, 'I have kept all these since my youth.' And do you know what he had the audacity to say then? Do you?" Again David was almost yelling, his face scorched with anger.

"For goodness sake, David," responded the amused and yet bewildered Jeremiah. "What on earth did this Jesus say that so upsets you?"

"You'll remember what I said earlier about selling all my possessions. Well, that's not all he said. You just listen to all that he said to me. He said, he said, 'There is still one thing lacking. Sell all that you own and distribute the money to the poor, and you will have treasure in heaven; then come, follow me.'"

"And?" asked Jeremiah.

"And I turned and left. I was terribly disappointed with his answer," replied David with a faraway look in his eyes.

"Well, I'm relieved at that," Jeremiah said with a laugh. "I'd be without a job, and you'd be without your idol."

"What do you mean 'You'd be without your idol'? Are you suggesting that money is my god? Why, I am a faithful Jew. I attend synagogue without fail; I'm a student of the Torah; I give of my means according to the law, as much as thirty percent; and I deal fairly with all of my customers. Jeremiah, you keep up that kind of talk, and you'll be looking for a job." David spoke with a forced certainty, for a doubt about his own life had entered his heart.

"All right, all right, forget what I said," Jeremiah protested, looking down all the while. "I was only joking."

David stood still. The arrow had struck its mark with absolute precision. He thought again about Jesus' remarks to him and realized that Jesus had challenged the center of his life. He thought, *Jesus listed the social commandments without asking about* the first: " . . . *you shall have no other gods before me."* David shook himself, speaking out loud, "This is crazy. I'm no idol worshipper. Why am I so disturbed by the peasant thoughts of an itinerate rabbi? They're wandering over the land in large numbers."

Jeremiah heard David's remarks, but remained silent. He, too, had been struck with self-doubt about his own life. The thought impinged upon his mind, *I wonder if this could be the Messiah? Oh, come on, I'm thinking crazy thoughts. Why on earth would I attach the ravings of a local rabbi with the Messiah?*

Weeks and months passed, but the searching look of Jesus' eyes would not leave David, nor would Jesus' instructions desert his memory. Sometimes at night, David woke with Jesus' face before him. At other times, an alluring gold idol danced through his dreams, mocking his life and commitment to God.

Jeremiah, too, was troubled. He often had to shake himself out of deep contemplation about his own life and the identity of Jesus. He said nothing to his boss about the matter for fear that David might dismiss him, but Jeremiah noticed that David was unusually subdued and pensive.

One day as Passover was rapidly approaching, David turned to Jeremiah as they worked together over the business accounts, "Shall we go to Jerusalem together as is our custom?"

"I certainly planned to go with you, David," Jeremiah said.

"Do you want to travel with other pilgrims or alone as usual?" asked David.

"To tell you the truth, I'd feel much better traveling with others. There have been too many robberies and beatings on the road to Jerusalem for us to go alone," said Jeremiah thoughtfully.

"I agree," said David. "We'll go with Zechariah and Malachi and their friends."

The journey to Jerusalem was uneventful; but as the pilgrims reached the outskirts of the city, they began hearing stories of Jesus' presence and actions in Jerusalem. Talk abounded that this Jesus was the Messiah and had come to establish the Kingdom of God on Zion. Some of the Zealots who worked the crowds were anticipating a chance to participate in a revolt against the Romans. The Pharisees were trying to temper the enthusiasm with warnings about the nearness of Roman legions. But nothing could stem the flood of stories pouring out of the city about this rabbi, who could defeat the Scribes in debate, silence the Sadducees, and embarrass the Pharisees.

David and Jeremiah lodged with friends who told of Jesus' driving the money changers from the temple and of his miraculous healings. Both David and Jeremiah were intrigued by the stories, and they decided to find this Jesus and listen to his teachings. They tried repeatedly to get close to Jesus, but the crowds kept them at such a distance they could hear only bits and pieces of what Jesus said.

On Friday morning, the two friends received the news that Jesus had been arrested. When David heard the charges of sedition and blasphemy, he said, "Jeremiah, I thought this might happen. Another dreamer and troubler of Israel is about to die."

"David, how can you say that?" responded Jeremiah. "You don't know enough to dismiss Jesus that easily."

"The fool told me to sell all my goods. Didn't he?" ejaculated David. "I should have known at that moment that this Jesus was beside himself. Besides, nothing good comes from Galilee," he said with a dismissive smile.

Jeremiah didn't respond. Suddenly, he felt compelled to find Jesus. "David, I'm going to find out what has happened to Jesus."

"What? Don't be a fool!" David spoke through a cruel laugh.

"Fool or not, I'm going," said Jeremiah as he turned to leave.

"All right, I'll go with you," said David abruptly.

The search led the pair to the Praetorian of Pilate. There they joined the crowd watching Jesus' inquisition. When Pilate asked whether to release Barabbas or Jesus, the crowd cried out to release Barabbas. And when Pilate asked what to do with Jesus, David shouted along with the crowd, "Crucify him, crucify him!"

Jeremiah turned squarely into David's face, shook him, and demanded, "How can you call for any man's crucifixion, much less for Jesus' death?"

David jerked himself away from Jeremiah's grasp and hissed, "I almost threw away my fortune for that holy man. I almost followed him. And if I had, where would I be now, but poor and on the run from the authorities?" David then turned to jeer and laugh at Jesus along with the crowd as the soldiers led him away to Golgotha.

Jeremiah followed quietly, wondering with a fevered mind why he was so drawn to a man convicted of capital crimes. He watched the crucifixion with David, an unbridgeable gulf growing between them, staying until Jesus was dead. As he watched Jesus die, he knew the truth. As crazy as it seemed, Jesus was God's Messiah.

As Jeremiah and David turned from the cross, David mocked, "The end of another messiah. Good riddance! And to think, I almost . . ."

"Yes, I know," said Jeremiah bitterly, "you almost gave up your idol for Jesus."

"I'll not have you say that again," shouted David. "I'm no idol worshipper."

"David, we both have been idol worshippers. I loved money just as much as or even more than you. I coveted your business and was even tempted to cheat you to create my own wealth." Jeremiah knew that he had just lost his job, but it didn't matter.

"You what? You were thinking of stealing from me to get rich? You ingrate," croaked David. "Get out of my sight and out of my life!"

"David, I never stole from you," said Jeremiah quietly, "but I have so worshipped money that I easily could have."

David, fists clenched as if to strike, shouted, "Get away from me!"

Jeremiah turned from David and headed into Jerusalem. He had to find someone who knew Jesus in order to learn more. He thought, *This morning, I had a friend and a bright future. This afternoon, I have alienated my friend and lost my job. In fact, I have only enough money for a few days of food and lodging. Well, Jesus, I come just as I am. Perhaps David is right. I'm a fool.*

The Rabbi

The little village was alive with activity before Passover, despite the unusual heat that had gripped the land. Small groups of people were gathered here and there along the main street, and everyone seemed to be talking at the same time. The last time there had been this much excitement, a garrison of Roman soldiers had camped just outside the town, entering only to steal the villagers' supplies. Rebekah didn't know what to make of all this activity. Fearing the unknown, she ran to talk to her mother.

"Mother, are the soldiers coming back to hurt us?" asked Rebekah.

"No, child, a new rabbi and his disciples are coming to the village tomorrow," assured Naomi.

"But rabbis come here all the time. We respect them as our teachers, but I've never seen people act this way before," offered Rebekah thoughtfully.

"But Jesus is a special rabbi," said her mother. "People who have seen him talk about his love and how he teaches with authority, using as examples things the ordinary people will understand. Even the children are drawn to him because of the way he teaches." Naomi's eyes were dancing with excitement as she talked.

"Will I be able to see him and talk to him?" asked Rebekah, catching her mother's joy.

"I don't know, Rebekah," mused Naomi. "You'll be able to see him, but with all the men pressing to listen and question him, I don't know if he'll have time for women and children." Naomi's spirits dropped a bit. *Why aren't the women allowed to study the Torah and participate in the discussions?* thought

Naomi. *Just once I wish someone would acknowledge that we have minds.* She turned to her daughter. "Enough talk, Rebekah. We have a lot to do to get ready for Jesus' coming. You had better be about your chores."

The new day dawned bright and cool, but heat lurked behind each breeze. Rebekah was up early to get a look at the new rabbi, dressed in her finest clothes. Breakfast came and went, but nothing happened. Rebekah was about to give up on this rabbi when she heard running feet just outside her window, followed by a shout, "He's here!"

By the time Naomi and Rebekah got to where Jesus was teaching, the men had crowded in and were listening intently. The women and children lingered at the back of the crowd. Fortunately, the people were seated, allowing Naomi and Rebekah to see and hear Jesus.

"But from the beginning of creation, God made them male and female," taught Jesus. "For this cause a man shall leave his father and mother, and the two shall become one flesh; consequently they are no longer two, but one flesh. What therefore God has joined together, let no man separate."

Rebekah did her best to follow the teaching, but found it to be grown-up talk. She did like the way Jesus spoke, gently and openly. Rebekah thought his face was like the children she played with: bright, interested, and smiling. Rebekah liked this Jesus very much.

After Jesus finished teaching and answering the many questions raised by the elders of the community, a mother started toward Jesus with her child, seeking a blessing for her little boy.

"Stop here, woman," said a disciple named Andrew. "We don't allow children near the teacher. He's too busy."

Rebekah watched the incident and decided that Jesus was no different from all the other rabbis. Women and children were not allowed to interfere.

"Permit the children to come to me; do not hinder them," said Jesus, "for the kingdom of God belongs to such as these."

Rebekah could hardly believe her ears. Her mother took her by the arm and started toward the rabbi. And as if in a dream, she felt herself in the arms of Jesus.

"Child, God loves you and so do I," said Jesus.

Just as Jesus let her down, Rebekah blurted out, "I am a girl, but I want to be your disciple."

"And so you shall be, Rebekah, so you shall," said Jesus through a bright grin that filled Rebekah's heart with joy.

Jesus left the next morning on his way to Jerusalem for Passover, and Rebekah ran with the crowd to say good-bye to him. She stood watching for a long time until he and his disciples were out of sight. Rebekah had never been to Jerusalem, but she had heard of the beautiful temple that had been built by Herod the Great.

As Passover approached, Naomi called Rebekah to her. "Rebekah, we are going to Jerusalem for Passover. Uncle Nicodemus has invited us to the Seder at his home."

"Oh, Mother, I've wanted to go to Jerusalem ever since I heard from visiting rabbis about the temple and how the city looks to the pilgrims as they approach—like 'a jewel in the sun'—they said. Does it look like a jewel, Mother?"

"I don't know, Rebekah," laughed her mother, "but we'll both know in a few days."

"Jesus is going to be there, Mother," said Rebekah, remembering his visit. "Can we go see him?"

"Rebekah, Jerusalem will be filled with so many people that a chance meeting with Jesus is not likely," responded her mother. "You really love Jesus, don't you?"

"He made me feel like I mattered—like he really loved me," responded Rebekah.

"Yes, he did," added Naomi.

As Passover approached, Rebekah could hardly contain the excitement she felt. Every day seemed to go by more slowly than the day before. The hours dragged by as if she were walking with a weight too heavy to carry.

Finally, the day came, and Rebekah and her mother went to Jerusalem. They were a part of a group from the village, as traveling alone was unsafe. They sang Psalms as they traveled, and Rebekah's favorite was Psalm 100: "Shout joyfully to the Lord, all the earth. Serve the Lord with gladness; come before him with joyful singing. Know that the Lord himself is God; it is he who has made us, and not we ourselves; we are his people and the sheep of his pasture."

The pilgrims were singing as they topped a hill overlooking Jerusalem, and the group fell silent as they saw the beauty of the holy city of God. The light reflecting off the marble surface of the Temple was rose-colored in the afternoon light and looked like it had reflected off the surface of water.

"Mother, it *is* a jewel!" shouted Rebekah. "It *is* a jewel!"

"Yes, child, it is God's jewel," her mother said softly.

As Naomi and Rebekah entered the city, the crowds became thicker until the streets were filled. Naomi clutched Rebekah's hand and pushed her way to the house of Uncle Nicodemus. They were relieved to get out of the crush.

Uncle Nicodemus was an important man in Jerusalem, a member of the Jewish court called the Sanhedrin. As the family took the Passover together, Nicodemus mentioned a disturbance centered on a rabbi named Jesus. He expressed concern that if certain members of the court had their way, Jesus would be crucified as an enemy of Israel.

Rebekah, hearing Jesus' name, interrupted the Seder, "I want to see Jesus. I love him. He is good."

"You know this Jesus, Rebekah?" asked her uncle.

"Yes, Uncle Nicodemus, he blessed me when he came to our village," responded Rebekah, realizing she had interrupted the Passover Seder. "What does it mean to crucify someone?"

"Rebekah, it is a way of taking the life of a criminal," said Nicodemus sadly.

"But he isn't a criminal. He is a good man, and I love him," cried Rebekah, getting to her feet. "How could anyone hurt a man like Jesus?"

"Child, I love him too, for I met and had a discussion with him. Never have I known a man like him. Yet there are people who are threatened by his goodness. They are afraid of losing their power over the people," responded Nicodemus.

"Uncle Nicodemus, you must do something," Rebekah said, choking back the tears. "You must *do* something!" Rebekah ran from the room weeping.

Nicodemus followed Rebekah and held her to him. "Rebekah, I'll do all that I can to save him from death."

Despite Nicodemus's efforts, Jesus was condemned and crucified. The loving rabbi who revealed God to his people was treated as a criminal.

When Nicodemus came home about mid-afternoon, he told Naomi and Rebekah that Jesus was dead. Rebekah cried, and her mother sat in stunned silence.

"Rebekah," said Nicodemus softly, "Joseph of Arimathea and I are going to bury him in a new tomb. Jesus had no money, but we cannot let such a one go without proper burial. I want you to know that I tried my best to save his life, but no one would listen."

Rebekah did not respond, but rose from her chair and went to her room.

After the Sabbath was over on Saturday evening, Rebekah approached her uncle and asked, "Will you take me to the grave of Jesus so that I can say good-bye and leave a flower?"

Nicodemus looked at his niece a long time and said, "Yes, Rebekah, I'll take you there tomorrow morning."

Just after dawn, Nicodemus and Rebekah went to Jesus' grave. As they approached, Nicodemus became very angry. The stone was rolled away. "How could the soldiers let robbers enter this grave and steal its contents!" he shouted angrily. He ran to the door of the tomb and found it empty. He entered and sat down, considering what to do next.

Rebekah stood alone—crying—some distance from the tomb. She had dropped the flowers she had brought to put at the grave.

"Rebekah, Rebekah," said a voice behind her. Rebekah turned and found herself looking into the face of a kneeling Jesus. She ran to him and threw herself into his arms. "I thought they had killed you, but you're alive!"

"Rebekah, I did die, but my Father in heaven raised me from the dead," said Jesus. "I'll not explain all about this now, but I am alive. You'll understand why I had to die in the years to come. Just believe in me as the resurrected one."

"I do believe you," said Rebekah. "But I don't understand."

"Rebekah, you remember my visit to your village, how I came and stayed a little while and had to leave. Well, because I'm resurrected, I can be with you and never leave you. You won't see me, but I'll be there. Wherever you go, I'll be at your side."

"But I see you now. Why won't I see you?" said Rebekah.

"I've been changed by my Father so that I will no longer be limited as an ordinary man. I'll be able to be with all my disciples everywhere, all of the time," Jesus said this with the same wide smile he had given Rebekah at her village.

"But I won't be able to talk with you, Jesus," said Rebekah.

"But you can talk with me anytime you choose. I'll be listening to every word," said Jesus lovingly. "Rebekah, I must be on my way to be with the rest of my disciples."

Rebekah watched as Jesus walked out of sight, but she felt no loss. For she knew that Jesus was with her, and would be forever.

Rebekah remembered her Uncle Nicodemus and went to the grave. "Come out, Uncle Nicodemus, let's go home," said Rebekah calmly.

Nicodemus looked closely at his niece. "Rebekah, you seem so peaceful. How can this be?"

"I've seen him. Jesus is resurrected!" responded Rebekah with a smile. And she took her surprised uncle by the hand and led him back home.

Closed Forever

"Centurion, go and find Claudius," Pilate commanded with a dismissive wave of his hand.

"As you command, Honorable Governor," responded the soldier. Immediately the centurion inquired about Claudius's whereabouts from the court officials and was told he was at a crucifixion on Golgotha. "Golgotha!" grumbled the centurion loudly as he turned to go. "Will these stinking Jews ever get enough of their messiahs and rebellions? We've killed enough Jews on crosses to fatten every buzzard in a hundred stadia, and we've let enough blood to turn the Jordan putrid." The court officials nodded, laughing at the thought of this soldier pushing his way through Jerusalem's streets, crowded with four to five times as many Jews as usual because of the Passover celebration.

Taking two trusted members of his cohort with him to protect himself from assassins, the centurion pushed, shoved, and trampled his way through the crowds and one of Jerusalem's gates, up to where three crosses stood on the *place of the skull*. "Claudius! The governor wants you back at his quarters."

"Good, I'm ready to get away from this filthy place," growled Claudius. "But first I have to take care of some unfinished business. Go over there and bring me that centurion of the Temple guards who is responsible for this crucifixion."

"Yes, Honorable Claudius, I'm at your service," responded a surprised centurion. "Should I tell him there is a problem?"

"Tell him nothing! Just bring him here at once."

The soldier in charge of the crucifixion approached warily and saluted crisply. "Sir, what does the Honorable Claudius require?"

"I heard your exclamation that this, this Jesus, this King of the Jews, is a Son of God. I wasn't the only one who heard what you said. The Jewish leaders heard it and are very upset. Do you want to cause a riot and perhaps lose your life and your status in the military?

Are you a disciple of this Jesus?" said Claudius in a tone dripping with sarcasm and contempt.

"Honorable Claudius, I lead men in battle, and I have seen many men die. I've crucified hundreds of Jews, but I've never seen a man die like this."

"'I've never seen a man die like this,'" mocked Claudius. "He bled, choked, lost control of his waste, groaned in agony, and died. What's so unusual about that?"

"I don't know, sir," said the centurion softly. "I don't know."

"'You don't know'? If you don't get a hold of yourself, you're going to be relieved of your responsibilities and made a common foot soldier. Do you understand?" Claudius was right in the centurion's face as he spoke.

"Yes, Honorable Claudius, I do understand, and I ask to be relieved of this barbaric duty, this feast of blood. I've had enough of Roman justice when it takes the life of the innocent, and surely this man was innocent!"

"Get back to the barracks and take your place among the common soldiers! And be thankful that I don't charge you with treason!" spat Claudius in a rage.

The former centurion stood saluting Claudius and thinking about Jesus and the mystery of his experience. *At least they can't take my thoughts from me. I must know more about this noble man, no matter the personal cost.* Looking back at the lifeless body on the center cross for the last time, he started toward the barracks.

Then Pilate's messenger to Claudius asked with a jeer, "Is that the King of the Jews," pointing to the man on the central cross, "and are those beside him his ministers of finance?"

Claudius roared with laughter, finally forcing out the fact that they were two common thieves. "Very good, centurion, 'ministers of finance.' That's certainly appropriate enough."

"What are all those women doing around here?" asked the messenger.

"They're his followers, I'm told," Claudius responded with a wink.

"A real ladies' man, was he? A desert monarch with his own personal harem," mocked the centurion. "I think I recognize one of the women. She may have served at one of our feasts . . . if you know what I mean?"

"Nothing proud about him," observed Claudius drily. He turned abruptly. "I'm going back."

"Do you want me to remain here to replace the demoted centurion?" asked the messenger, trying to score points for promotion.

"I do not. You will escort me back. I don't need a knife in the back from some zealot looking to make a name for himself," snapped Claudius.

"What if his disciples show up to cause a disturbance? There are rumors that he had a large following."

"Cowards, the whole lot of them, except for the women. With such friends, this Jesus didn't need enemies. A little public outcry, a flash of the broadsword, and his followers ran for cover like quail," scoffed Claudius. "Come on. Let's get back before too late. I don't need to face an angry Pilate."

After a wearisome trip through the Passover crowds in Jerusalem, Claudius stood before Pilate. Pilate, a hardened veteran of the Roman political system, looked with impatience on his stocky assistant, who coupled cynicism with an even temper and hid his lack of respect behind a practiced charm. Pilate, though a cynic as well, lacked Claudius's easy temperament and wasted no time on charm when a blow to the face or the ego would serve as well. He was as wiry as Claudius was squat and had a face that seemed eyeless. He was a disturbing presence.

Claudius stepped forward with eyes painted open on a closed soul. "You commanded my presence, Honorable Governor?" Claudius asked, as he bowed a bit extremely.

"Is he dead?" shot Pilate.

"Is who dead, Your Honor?"

"Who? You idiot! Is that Jew, Jesus, dead, of course!" replied Pilate angrily.

Claudius smiled to himself at having provoked his superior. "Jesus is dead."

"Are you sure, Claudius?"

"Dead as Herod the Great. The worms will have him in a few hours."

"How do you know he is dead?" urged Pilate.

"Because he quit breathing," Claudius flatly replied, playing now with his adversary.

"Insolent ass! 'He quit breathing.' Did you break his legs or lance him?"

"His legs were not broken. There was no reason. A guard pierced his side, and blood and water, which had settled in his belly, poured out. He is dead." Claudius's tone had become totally professional.

"I'm glad he is dead. All I need is to have an ongoing dispute with the chief priest, his whole family, and the Sanhedrin. Being stuck in this wasteland post on the edge of the empire hasn't done my career any good, and a riot or a report to Caesar by disgruntled Jews won't help matters." Pilate's voice betrayed deep bitterness.

"Well, you can thank me for saving us from controversy when I visited the crucifixion. The centurion in charge was heard to exclaim that Jesus was "God's Son." I shut him up before his comment caused a riot. Just imagine a report to the Caesar that the Romans supported Jesus' claims. We would have been up on charges ourselves," observed Claudius smugly.

"Where is the centurion now?" asked Pilate.

"He's in the barracks and taking up his duties as a common soldier," laughed Claudius.

"Excellent! But keep an eye on this fool," ordered Pilate.

"Your Excellency, it's over. This Jesus will not bother us again. Take my word for it. He is dead and so is his movement," assured Claudius with an insidious purr.

"'It's over,' you say. How easily claimed. Nothing is ever over with in this land of Jehovah. Nothing! We crucify a thousand Jews for sedition or insurrection and another thousand take their places. Let them all go to hell. Just get me out of here!"

Claudius perceived that Pilate was troubled about this crucifixion. The soldier was completely baffled. "Honorable Governor, we have crucified hundreds and hundreds of Jews. Others wore the name of Jesus and died in the name of God and freedom. What is different this time?"

"I'll tell you what is different. Every seditionist rebel who stood before me would have spit on me if possible. They hate us, Claudius, and would kill us in a minute. This Jesus of Nazareth had no hate in him. When I asked him if he was King of the Jews, he said, 'You say so.' And when he was bitterly and, I might add, falsely accused, he said nothing. Not one word to his accusers. He didn't even hate them. When the crowds, encouraged by the temple authorities, finally cried out for his death and even exchanged him for a ruthless criminal named Barabbas, he stood like a soldier at his post. And my wife sent me a very troubling message, warning me to have nothing to do with this man's death. I was so touched by his presence and my wife's message that I symbolically washed my hands of his blood. Still, I feel that I shall never be free of his blood."

"Well, if you thought him innocent, why didn't you release him?" Claudius countered, already knowing the answer.

"Because I didn't want to provoke these precious citizens of the empire. I refuse to commit political suicide for a Jew, no matter how innocent."

"It's over, I tell you! In a few days this *King* of the Jews will be forgotten, along with the other enemies of Rome," said Claudius, momentarily irritated. "Or, do you believe he was a king or the Son of God?"

"I believe in nothing and no one, but whoever is in power at the moment," rasped Pilate.

"You are in power, Honorable Governor," cooed Claudius, recovering his balance.

"Yes, and don't forget it," replied Pilate. "Ah, and, Claudius, put a detail of soldiers out to follow Barabbas. I don't want that criminal free for very long. Let him taste just enough freedom to miss it all the more when we put him back in chains."

As Claudius was leaving, he noticed a member of the Sanhedrin waiting to see Pilate. *Probably here to thank the governor for his quick action in the matter of Jesus of Nazareth versus the Sanhedrin,* thought Claudius.

"Honorable Pilate, I have come to make a request. A few friends and I want to take the body of Jesus and bury it. There will be no expense to the state, and the burial will be private and without incident."

"Are you a follower, Nicodemus? It was your court that wanted him dead. You can't be very popular if you favor him."

"I'm doing my duty for a fellow rabbi and Jew," responded Nicodemus respectfully.

"Doing your duty, are you? No, I tell you that you are his follower and you honor him," spoke Pilate knowingly.

"As you wish, Honorable Governor. I only ask you to act quickly, for the Sabbath will soon begin," urged Nicodemus.

"Take him. Please, be my guest. Let's have an end to this as soon as possible."

"Thank you, Honorable Governor," replied Nicodemus, starting to turn away.

The desperate bitterness of Pilate's tone made Nicodemus turn back to face him again. "Mark my words, pious Jew. Once he is in the tomb, there will be no escape," gloated Pilate. "Justice and injustice are the same to the dead, and the worms don't care. Put him in a sealed tomb and the matter of Jesus of Nazareth is closed. Closed forever. Do you hear me, Jew? Closed forever!"

New Beginnings

Pastor Roberts was feeling depressed as he sat in his office and worked on Advent and Christmas services. The past year had not been a good one for the pastor, or so he thought. He had always been acutely aware of a sense of call to be a pastor; but after a quarter of a century in the ministry, this had faded and, along with it, his usual sense of effective service to Christ.

As Pastor Roberts sat staring at a blank paper on which a sermon was to be written, he felt empty, worn, gospel-less, and somewhat sorry for himself. *Advent,* he thought, *is a time for new beginnings, the coming of Christ, and being embraced by God through the incarnation. Who am I kidding? It's the same old world with its broken people, including me. Beginnings? I'm beginning to see the hopeless condition of the world, the grip of sin, and the year-by-year sameness of all our arrogant meanness.* The pen in his hand stood motionless on the paper and caused a large black stain to spread gradually on the page. He looked at the Rorschach-like inkblot and felt somehow justified in his bitterness and lostness.

So immersed in his self-pity was he that Pastor Roberts failed to notice the office door open and a little person enter.

"Hello, Pastor," said Ruthie, "I just wanted to ask you a question."

Oh, boy, thought the pastor, *this is all I need, another interruption. I'm in the middle of preparing all these Advent services, and I've got to stop to answer silly questions. Great! Just great!*

"Yes, Ruthie, what is your question?" the pastor asked grumpily.

As Ruthie slipped into a chair near the desk, she asked innocently, "Are you mad at me?"

"Why do ask that?" replied the troubled pastor.

"You don't talk the same, Pastor," said Ruthie sadly.

"What do you mean?" queried the shaken minister, knowing full well what had caused the child's response.

"You're always ready to talk to me when I come, but . . . ," Ruthie hesitated, "but you don't . . ." Without ending the sentence, she slipped out of the chair and started toward the door.

"Wait, child," said the pastor. "I'm sorry about seeming to be mad at you. I really wasn't, but I was very distracted. Now what was your question?"

As she returned to the chair, the pastor took a close look at the little girl. Her brown hair was slightly askew, even though a red ribbon tried to keep it under control; and her brown eyes seemed to draw the pastor in as he was drawn into mud puddles when he was a child with new shoes. And right in the middle of a round face was a cute little nose just slightly left bearing. Her smile showed two front teeth seeking a final fit, giving her smile such an infectious quality that it caused a responding grin on the pastor's face. Combine such a face with a pudgy, but active, body; and Pastor Roberts was helpless to resist no matter how he was feeling.

"Why is the green thing you wear around your neck on Sunday changed to purple?" Ruthie hurriedly asked. "And why are the other green things changed to purple?"

"Oh, you're talking about my stole and the paraments," chuckled the pastor, feeling better in spite of himself.

"Why are they purple?" persisted Ruthie.

"Purple or blue is used at this time of the year, because we just finished the season of Trinity, and we are entering Advent," responded Reverend Roberts.

Ruthie sat very still, looking somewhat baffled. She tried to respond, but nothing seemed to make sense. She really didn't understand about Trinity and Advent.

Pastor Roberts realized how he must have sounded and started again, "Ruthie, the purple tells us that we are preparing for Christ's coming into the world."

"But I thought Jesus has already come," said Ruthie. "We talk that way every Sunday in church school."

"Good for you, Ruthie," the pastor responded. "You're exactly right, but there's more to it than that. Advent is about Christ's coming to us in three ways. Christ did come in the flesh when he was born of Mary in Bethlehem, lived among human beings, and died on the cross. But remember, Jesus was resurrected unto life. As our living Lord, he comes to us each day to minister to us and to help us live for him. And on some future date, Jesus will come to take all his children home to be with him forever. Does that explain things, Ruthie?"

Ruthie was trying to sort out the meaning of this adult talk and took quite a while to answer. "I guess, Pastor. It's nice to know Jesus is my friend. So when I see the purple thing around your neck, I know my friend is coming. Is that right?"

"Ruthie, your understanding is better than my explanation. You've got it," said the pastor, grinning from ear to ear.

"Besides, I really like purple and wish we could have that color all the time," Ruthie said with a smile. She got out of the chair, pulled open the office door, and started out. "Good-bye, Pastor," she said, and skipped out of the office and down the hall.

As Pastor Roberts watched her go, he knew what had been wrong during the past few months. He had forgotten that Jesus came, Jesus is near, and Jesus is coming. He had forgotten that Jesus is his friend.

"And a little child shall lead them . . ." crossed his lips as he prayed for the Lord to help him.

He looked down at the ink-stained paper on his desk, crumpled it up, and threw it away. It was time for new beginnings.

The Shepherds

"It was the wind, and that's all it was," said Isaac with a scowl on his face that came through his voice. When Isaac spoke, people listened attentively; because Isaac was about six feet five inches tall with broad powerful shoulders, sculpted features, pockmarked face, and dark burning eyes. Usually, there was no protest of disagreement for fear of the consequences, but this time was different.

"No, Isaac, it was not the wind," replied Jacob, standing a full foot shorter than Isaac and possessing a physical presence akin to David standing before

Goliath. "We heard voices that were the most beautiful we've ever heard, voices like sweet music from the harp, or like the gentle sound made by a bubbling brook."

"Bubbling waters, is it, music from a harp? More like sounds coming from raving madmen if you ask me," said Isaac, drawing himself up to full height. "Or maybe you're leftovers from the Tower of Babel."

"Go ahead and make fun of us if you must, but we heard the voices and saw the glory of God," said Andrew, who was even less a presence than Jacob, launching words on a voice that was a bit too high to be taken seriously by Isaac. But his absolute sincerity had a force of its own.

"And you saw the glory of the Lord too?" scoffed Isaac. Pray tell me what the Lord looked like; for I've been wandering these hills for twenty years, and I've never seen God or God's glory and don't expect to."

"Isaac, we didn't see God. We saw what must have been his glory surrounding us and the sheep. We . . . we were so terrified by what we saw and heard that we tried to hide among the rocks," explained Nehemiah, an imposing man in his own right, but less of a presence than Isaac.

"First, you tell me that you heard voices that sounded like a bubbling water or beautiful music from a harp, but now you're talking about being terrified and hiding among the rocks. Which is it going to be? If you know!" laughed Isaac. "All you heard was the wind and saw a shooting star, and they have become the Lord and voices of—let me guess—his angels. While you continue to spin this yarn, why don't you tell me what the angels said."

Malachi, who was sitting some distance away from the discussion, moved closer and intervened. He wore the typical dress of the shepherd: robe, rough but sturdy sandals, a head covering that extended down the back of his neck; and he carried an old staff that had been his father's. Burned by the sun and wind, he bore rugged, bearded features and stringy, matted hair. Shorter than Isaac, Malachi compensated by a powerful voice and assertive presence. "As for being afraid, yes, we were afraid. We felt such awe that we had to hide ourselves from the visiting presence, and we do know what the angels said," Malachi replied. "They said, 'Glory to God in the highest heaven, and on earth peace among those whom he favors!'"

"That's just terrific! 'Peace on earth' for shepherds living in a land controlled by a crazy and violent King Herod and surrounded by legions of the Roman army. If you saw anything with wings, it must have been Roman eagles, not angels. Wonderful, just wonderful! I'm out here in the wilderness with a bunch of nuts, practical jokers, or liars," responded Isaac with growing anger.

Malachi stepped forward almost touching Isaac and, lifting himself to every inch of height he could manage, looked at him eye to eye in the light of the campfire. "Isaac, the angels said something else. They said, 'Do not be afraid; for see—I am bringing you good news of great joy for all the people: to you is born this day in the city of David a Savior, who is the Messiah, the Lord. This will be a sign to you: you will find a child wrapped in bands of cloth and lying in a manger.' We were all there, and we heard these things."

"The Messiah in a manger? God's Messiah born in a stable in Bethlehem? Messages from angels and God's glory shining down on poor shepherds in the Judean hills? Well, I don't believe any of this," said Isaac coldly, staring back at Malachi, so close that their noses almost touched. "Next thing you'll tell me is that you are headed to Bethlehem to find, to find, this . . . this savior and leave me here with the sheep."

The other shepherds looked at each other knowingly, for they had already decided to go to Bethlehem before Isaac had returned to their camp.

Malachi, who had become spokesman for the group, said, "We are going to Bethlehem to find the

Messiah. How can we do anything else after what we have seen and heard?"

"Go ahead and chase your illusion, for that's all it is," shouted back Isaac. "I'll stay with the sheep and have better company than the lot of you."

As the little band of shepherds traveled toward the city of David, doubt began to set in as might be expected given the force of Isaac's awful skepticism. "Are you sure we heard voices?" asked Jacob. "I was so sure until Isaac began to question and mock us."

"And the light. What was the light if not the glory of God?" asked another one.

"Perhaps it was the moon or a falling star, and maybe the voices were just the sound of the wind moving over the hillside. You all know the strange sounds that can occur in the dead of night," responded another. "After all, why would God have anything to do with outcasts like us?"

The shepherds had almost convinced themselves to return to their flocks when Malachi pointed out that they were too close to Bethlehem to turn back now. "We're here. Why not look around and see what we find?"

"Look where? There must be thousands more people in this area than is usual because of the census, and there must be mangers all over this area," observed Jacob. "Malachi, since you're leading this expedition, why don't you find the manger?" The other shepherds, descending deeper into doubt minute by minute, just laughed at Jacob's suggestion, nodding their heads.

"I don't know where to look," said Malachi, "but we can try to find the babe and his parents. Let's start at the local inn and ask the landlord if he knows of any pregnant women that are in this area. That can't hurt, can it? If we don't find them soon, we'll get back to the sheep and have a good laugh about the whole thing."

"Jewish women are always pregnant," said one of the shepherds with a guffaw. "That's like asking if the Romans collect taxes."

"All right, all right, you're not helping. Do you have a better suggestion?" asked an irritated Malachi. The response was silence. "I take it then that we try the innkeeper."

The shepherds gathered around the inn door like beggars looking for a handout, at least that's how the sleepy landlord saw them. "Get away from here, you mangy layabout! You're the second party to wake me from my sleep this night. Get away from here."

The shepherds turned to leave when Malachi was struck by the landlord's remark about another party of latecomers. Turning back before the innkeeper could shut and bolt the door, Malachi asked, "Was there a pregnant woman in the group that woke you earlier?"

"Yes, a very pregnant woman and, I suppose, her husband," shouted the landlord.

"Are they here in the inn?" called out Malachi to the further irritation of the innkeeper.

"Why do you care? Get away from here, or I'll raise the neighborhood."

"Are they here?" insisted another of the shepherds.

"The inn is full, but I told them they could use the stable in the back. Look there if you must. Just leave me alone," came the reply, punctuated by the slamming of the inn door.

The little group went behind the inn to a small stable in the rear, a shelter dug out of the side of a hill. Stumbling and cursing along a dark alley, they approached two figures, barely visible, huddling beside a manger. The man rose to meet them, staff in hand, readying himself physically to protect his family from attack.

"Stop! We have no money or goods that you would want," said the man.

"We didn't come to steal or to hurt you," responded Malachi, stopping his advance toward the little family.

"Then what are you doing here? Have you lost your way?" said a woman who was hidden by the darkness.

"I don't exactly know . . . I mean we know, but it doesn't make any sense to us," answered Malachi.

The man in the stable stepped out of the darkness and into the moonlight, warily addressing the shepherds, "What are you telling us? We don't understand any of this. We're just a poor family displaced because of the census requirements."

"First, let me ask if your wife gave birth to a baby this night?" queried Malachi in hushed tones, almost afraid of the answer. The other shepherds stared intently, waiting breathlessly for the answer.

"Yes . . . yes, she did. But how did you know, or, at least, why do you ask?"

"Earlier this evening, while we were watching our flocks in the nearby hills, we thought . . . well, we thought we heard angels and saw the glory of God. We were even convinced that we were sent here to find God's Messiah," said Malachi, now finding it difficult to believe his own words.

There was silence, a protracted silence, a deafening silence as if fixing the moment on the edge of eternity.

The man turned and spoke to the woman in the stable, "Mary, did you hear what the shepherd said?"

Mary responded pensively, as if remembering something important, that she had heard what the shepherd had said. Then she responded, "I was just recalling the angel Gabriel's visit with me, and how I believed, but struggled so deeply to understand."

"Can we see the child?" asked Jacob, his curiosity overwhelming him.

"The child is sleeping," responded Joseph.

"We left our flocks to search for a newborn child, and now that we have found one, we deeply need to look, if only for a moment. We will not disturb the little one," pressed Jacob.

"Gather quietly around the manger, for both the child and his mother are tired from the travail of giving birth," responded Joseph firmly.

"What is the child's name?" inquired Jacob.

"We named him 'Jesus' in keeping with the angel's instruction to Mary," replied Joseph.

The shepherds looked at each other, for they knew that "Jesus" meant God is salvation.

The shepherds gathered around the manger and saw a newborn infant that looked like a thousand other Jewish infants, but each shepherd experienced a persistent sense of joy, peace, and satisfaction. After silently watching the child for some time, they took their leave and started back to their flocks and a waiting, skeptical Isaac.

The shepherds traveled in silence until Malachi shattered it, "The Messiah of God in a manger in a stable. No one will believe this, but I do. I do believe, but it doesn't make sense. I mean, how can God send his King to poverty and into such obscurity? I don't understand. I don't."

The other shepherds began talking almost at once, adding their own experiences of faith and amazement and an abiding sense of peace. Each step they took on the road home seemed to be with a sense of deepening faith and joy.

Arriving back at their camp in the hills, they faced the smug countenance of Isaac, for he was thoroughly convinced that theirs had been a fool's errand. "Well, did you find the Messiah?"

Jacob was quick to respond, "Yes, we did!"

"You did, did you? Then tell me, did he look like God or an angel or a prophet? Did he glow in the dark or have a halo or wings? Perhaps he was surrounded by the glory of God."

"No, Isaac, the baby didn't have a halo or dwell in heavenly light. In fact, Jesus looked like other healthy newborn Jewish babies," responded Malachi gently. Malachi felt no need to get in Isaac's face or to raise his voice.

"I thought so," replied Isaac with a smirk. "There were no angels, no glory of God, and no Messiah, just another Jewish baby to discover the hardship of Israel's chosenness!"

One of the other shepherds looked at Isaac with the look of one at peace and said, "No, Isaac, we found the Messiah. We all believe that Jesus, as the baby was named, is our Lord."

"What proof do you have?" shot back Isaac. "You are all hardened shepherds. You have to see the world as it is, for only by doing so can you save your flocks from predators and robbers. Do you have some proof that I can believe?"

"No proof, Isaac, at least not the kind you want. But we are all sure that Jesus is the Messiah, and we each one came to this faith independently of the others. And, no, we can't exactly explain why." Malachi's voice was that of certain faith, not argument, a voice coming from inner conviction.

Isaac stood looking at his friends as if they were strangers, for he did not recognize them as the same shepherds who had left for Bethlehem just hours before. He was sure that they had become touched in the head by following their crazy sheep for too many years. "Is this what finally happens to shepherds after many years of loneliness?" he asked rhetorically. For him, that was the only possible answer that could explain the night's events. Isaac looked at his friends awhile longer and then turned away to see after his sheep.

The wind rose and whispered across the hills and valleys. Isaac drew his cloak around him and walked silently into the darkness.

And back in Bethlehem, a little Jewish family huddled in a dark stable and held each other against the cold.

—◄❖►—

Grandmother's Christmas Gift

"Doctor, how am I doing?" asked Grandmother Blackwell.

"Now, Esther, don't be worried," replied the heart specialist. "It's just another heart attack. By the way, how many does that make, four or five?"

At that exchange the family members that had gathered around her bed in High Point Memorial Hospital started to laugh. She had done it again. She had faced a life-threatening crisis and had beaten the odds. That was nothing new for my grandmother.

Grandmother had lost her husband in the flu pandemic of 1918. The flu had killed millions around the world and more soldiers than had bullets in World War I. The Blackwell home lost a husband and father of five children: Maddie, Vivien, Robert, James, and Richard, my father. Grandmother was left with five small children to raise, which was extraordinarily difficult by any measure; but this task was exacerbated by the crash of 1929, which further threatened her family which was already struggling to stay together. My father left high school just before graduating in order to get a job to help support the family. The other children did likewise. By hard work, pulling together, and the leadership of a strong mother, the family made it and produced five wonderful adults to take their places in society. Grandmother Blackwell had faced the terrible threats to her family and had beaten the odds.

Esther Blackwell was an imposing person to say the least. She was physically large and could fill a room with her presence. She had beautiful gray hair that was pulled back into a nicely coiffed bun. Her face was round with glowing cheeks and a clear complexion. Smiles and laughter had provided wrinkles that only enhanced her appearance. Bright, shining eyes, intelligent eyes, surveyed the world through rimless glasses and missed little of what was happening around her. She was always surprising her children and grandchildren with what she knew. Her attire was always neat and attractive, even if consisted of a simple housecoat and an apron.

Grandmother's infectious laughter was a joy to her family and friends. It seemed to spring from a source deep within her, rising up to fill a room, her home, and the lives of all around her. Sometimes, when I visited with my father, that laughter would precede her into the room, causing me to smile with anticipation. Grandmother's laughter was driven by a large intelligence and a marvelous sense of humor. Esther's sense of humor poked fun at herself, disarmed pretense, and turned tears into lenses through which to see life differently. Each of her children had a similar sense of humor and a readiness to laugh. Being present when the family gathered was a laugh riot, and I looked forward to such occasions throughout my young life. She taught us that a sense of humor was a powerful cure for the problems of life and that a sense of humor kept one from taking oneself too seriously.

Being around Grandmother Blackwell taught me a certainty of place, correct behavior, and a love for history. She openly made it clear what was expected of me, and her discipline was consistent and fair. She taught me the precious gift of family and the value of the family name. Grandmother made me aware of the family members who had fought in the Revolutionary War, the Civil War, and World Wars I and II. Respecting the roots of her family, she shared with me its history that reached back to England, early settlements of the Northeast, and our migration to the American South. *A certainty of place* that I wrote of earlier was a reference to family inclusion. I wasn't just a cute, or not so cute, grandchild to be hugged, kissed, and spoiled. I wasn't a toy to be played with and forgotten. Grandmother made sure that I was included in the family and its history. I had roots in the rootless world, and my identity was not provided by my peers, a street gang, or an amorphous cultural idea. I was a Blackwell with roots in England and the American South. I came from a Christian family, which was Baptist in practice, but ecumenical in spirit. Though I have from time to time temporarily misplaced my heritage, it has never been far away or without influence. So many children in our time seem bereft of the roots that strong family ties could remedy. What a shame it is that some people have no sense of identity except that provided by the latest fad. I am thankful that a loving and thoughtful Grandmother would not let that happen to me.

Grandmother Blackwell loved the Christmas season as much as any child or adult I have ever known. It was a season that suited her laughter, joy, and giving spirit. There was nothing more exciting than being around her as Christmas approached. In fact, I always made sure that I made one visit to Grandmother's before Christmas. You see, Grandmother had a Christmas tradition of making gifts for her children and grandchildren. Raising her children during a time of economic hardship meant that she seldom had money to buy them gifts. So she saved up the ingredients for baking and made cakes and cookies for her children at Christmas. She continued this act of love until age and physical decline made it impossible. At first, I didn't understand why she hadn't purchased a gift for me, but my father put me straight after hearing my complaint about Grandmother's gift. After having the matter explained to me, I was always grateful for her gifts, knowing that love was expressed in every piece of candy, slice of cake, and cookie.

Hence, there was one thing I truly enjoyed at Christmas more than any other. Every year just before Christmas, I went with my father during the time that Grandmother was in the midst of making her gifts. The smells in her house were beyond adequate description. Nutmeg wafted gently from the kitchen as pumpkin pies baked in the oven. A nutty, sweet smell blended with the nutmeg as pecan pies cooled on the breakfast nook table. The distinct and insistent odor of cinnamon and apples took its place in the pantheon of heavenly fragrances. The toasty presence of sugar cookies was unmistakable in the midst of all the baking, and the sweet elegance of chocolate fudge and divinity candy made their importance certain. Grandmother's wonderful sugar cake made my mouth water as it cooled and set on the back porch. But the crown for Christmas smells went to the warm ginger cakes and cookies displayed on the dining room table. Every time I get a whiff of that wonderful delicacy, I remember Grandmother Blackwell and the visits before Christmas. I could sit for hours in the living room in a fragrance-induced stupor while looking at the Christmas tree near the fireplace. Grandmother would always give me a piece of gingerbread to hold me until Christmas, but it never did. It just made the wait a little more bearable as I anticipated the fun of trying to get sugar cake off of my face.

But there was something else about those visits that ultimately left a deeper impression on me than the smells of cakes, cookies, pies, and candies. This something was the sound of love coming from Grandmother's kitchen. At first I didn't notice this sound, but as time went on, I became more and more aware of its presence. I could hear Grandmother gently laughing as she took one of her gifts from the oven, watched the setting of fudge, or waited on the slow cooling of her sugar cake. Sometimes, I could hear her grump as one of her productions didn't meet her standards—for love seeks perfect expression. At other times, she would feign disappointment that there wasn't enough fudge or cake to go around, meaning that she would just have to make another batch. How delighted she was! Listening to her labor in the kitchen taught me what it means to love one's work and the sounds that accompany works of love. The sheer joy that accompanied her time in the kitchen was the best gift that she could give or receive. How sad that much of what we do in life is loveless drudgery. How tragic it is that love of work and works of love seem to be disappearing.

When Christmas finally arrived, I watched with rapt attention as my father opened the gifts from my grandmother. A warmth seemed to fill the air as I received a piece of gingerbread or sugar cake, a warmth of love that flowed from my Grandmother Blackwell to her family. Most of the gifts that I have received in my life are long forgotten, but I shall never forget her gifts. Love is like that.

Another Spirit of Christmas

"In 1843, Charles Dickens published the now famous and beloved *A Christmas Carol*. You will remember the old miser Scrooge and the visits of the ghosts of Christmas Past, Present, and Future. You will also recall the happy ending for Tiny Tim and the Cratchits, not to mention Scrooge and his relatives. Lovely, just lovely! How sweet and sentimental, for Christmas makes everything right. Well, I'm the spirit of poverty, loneliness, despair, hunger, and rejection that walks among and inflicts the people of the streets, ghettos, and rural areas of this country. Come with me and visit one of my Christmas victims.

"Over there is Russell, who has been on the streets of Trenton for more than ten years. He ran away from his last foster home when he was twelve years old because of abuse. He's now about twenty-five, but looks fifty, sort of like a prune. I've done wonders with Russ by inflicting him mercilessly with pain of about every kind. 'Why is that?' you ask. Russell is black, and the unrelenting bigotry of the society allows me a free hand with people of color. Let's follow him around on Christmas Eve and Christmas Day. Look, over there. That's Russell's home."

"'Home?' That's a deserted lot covered with trash."

"But Russell's home, nevertheless. More specifically, he lives in that refrigerator box under a pile of debris that has been heaped up for protection against the elements. Snug, don't you think?"

"'Snug?' It's damp and smelly, not to mention cold and filthy. No human being should be forced to live in such conditions."

"Here comes Russell now. Boy, is he in for a surprise! That's a poacher who's going to evict Russell from his home. This ought to be fun to watch. More pain and misery, but let's listen."

"Hey, that's my home. Get away from here," demanded Russell.

"You just try and make me. You come on and I'll lay you out permanent with this pipe."

"I ain't got no weapon, but I got to have my box 'cause I'm sick." With that, Russell advanced on his antagonist and was dealt a glancing blow to the head, which opened a nasty wound and drove him back and to the ground. Bleeding and helpless, he crawled out of the lot to the street. He faced a very cold night with no hope of protection from the bitter wind.

"Why doesn't someone stop this and save Russell?"

"Who really cares what happens to Russell? He doesn't count in this society. He's a throwaway. He's as disposable as the garbage in that deserted lot."

"Look! What's he doing now?"

"Oh, he's trying to find an old rag to tie up his wound. There he's got it."

"But that's filthy. He'll infect the wound."

"So!"

"'So?' It'll kill him!"

"So?"

"But we can't let a person live like this."

"Oh, be real. They're everywhere on these streets."

"What, what's he doing now?"

"He's panhandling for money or food. Let's see how the good folks of Trenton respond during this Christmas season."

"Got a quarter for food?"

"Get away from me, you bum!"

"Ma'am, will you help me? I'm hungry and sick." The woman looked away from him without saying a word. He wasn't even worth a verbal rejection.

"Spirit, how can they ignore such obvious need?"

"The same way you do and have for years. You're my ally in the ruin and destruction of the street people."

"Where's he going?"

"Russell's making his way down to the soup kitchen for a hot meal. Mrs. James likes Russell and tries to give him a little extra food. She's speaking to him now."

"Hey, Russell, how are you doing? Heavens, what happened to your head? You ought to go to the emergency center. You look sick, Russell."

"Ma'am, they don't like our kind down at the hospital. They treat us like common dirt. Maybe I am."

"Hush up, Russell. That's no way to talk. If you won't go to the emergency room, then sit down and have some hot turkey and dressing. Have as much as you like."

"Could I get a little food to take with me tonight? It'll help me get through the night. It's real cold."

"Sure you can. Now eat slowly and rest here in the warmth. We don't close tonight until after midnight."

"Thank you, Mrs. James. Thank you."

"Spirit, where is Russell going now that the soup kitchen is closed?"

"To the streets, back to the bitter cold."

"He is stopping at the church. Surely, someone will help him."

"Russell likes the Christmas Eve service, especially the music."

"But why doesn't he go inside? The doors are not locked."

"Because the good folks inside will not welcome him, and he's had enough rejection for ten lifetimes. Why go where you aren't wanted?"

"That's not fair, not fair at all! Our church gives a few dinners at Christmas and a few gifts to help the indigent."

"You mean you salve your consciences by doing a few good deeds. If you really want to make a difference, provide sustained help to the homeless. But that will mean getting your hands dirty. God forbid!"

"Look. Where's he going now?"

"He's going to find some newspapers to put inside his clothes to protect him from the cold."

"Then, what?"

"He'll find a grate, a steam grate if he's lucky, and he'll lie down."

"But Russell is obviously hurt and sick. If he sleeps in the open tonight, he will probably die of exposure."

"And likely he will die. If not tonight, then another night."

"But I don't want Russell to die. No one should die in this way—cold, alone, rejected."

"Death is Russell's only real friend. When it comes, Russell's hunger, exposure, and rejection will be over."

"But . . ."

"But, what? What you want is a happy ending to Russell's story. That would make you feel better, wouldn't it? If you want happy endings so badly, why don't you learn what Christmas is really about, instead of burying it under all this sentimental rubbish that ultimately denies its truth?"

"I know what Christmas is about. It is about the birth of Jesus the Christ."

"Yes, but you keep Jesus in swaddling clothes and lying in a manger or buried under mounds of presents that mean nothing two days after Christmas. Jesus grew up to show you how to be a loving, caring human being. Jesus died on a cross for you and for your world. Jesus taught the way of selflessness and sacrificial love that would clear the streets of sick and lonely people."

"But Jesus himself said that we would always have the poor with us."

"Certainly, there will always be those who suffer in the world; but that is no excuse for not following the way of Jesus, the way of sacrificial love."

"Boy, do you ever need a dose of Christmas spirit!"

"You mean, like you have it? No, thanks! I'll stick with honest misery and rejection, rather than false piety and social blindness."

"I've got to get home. We open presents very early on Christmas."

"Merry Christmas!"

Russell found his steam grate and slept through the night, but was too ill to get up on Christmas Day. A policeman tried to chase him off the street, but discovered that Russell was too weak to move. Two days later, Russell died of pneumonia in Mercer Medical Center. He died alone except for one visitor. A man in ragged clothes stood by his bed to the very end of his suffering. When he turned to walk away, one could see scars on his brow and nail prints in his hands. He was weeping as he went back to the streets. His call is the same now as it was then, "Come and follow me."

A Little Old Donkey

"Get out of the way, old thing," said the stable owner to the little donkey. "You ain't worth a halfpenny anymore."

The little donkey dropped his head at the cruel judgment. Although he moved away to find comfort among the other animals, the phrase "old thing" kept pushing its way to the front of the little fellow's consciousness until it was a tinny sound in his ears.

A few years ago, he wouldn't have said that to me, thought the donkey. *I was one of the best pack animals ever known on the trade routes. Why, I could go all day under a full load of rich cloth, fragrant spices, gold and silver, and be ready for more.*

Just the thought of spices took the donkey back to the orient. Carrying spices was his favorite task, because the myrrh, frankincense, and cinnamon were truly delightful fragrances. After a long journey bearing these wonderful gifts of nature, the little donkey would carry the lingering smell in his hide for days.

Memories of spices and exotic journeys were suddenly broken by the stable owner's voice as he spoke to one of the stable boys, "That old feller 'll have to go soon. He's not able to work hard anymore, and he's just taking up room and eating food. We'll turn him out in the desert in a few days and let 'im fend for himself."

Please, please don't do that to me, agonized the donkey. *I'll die in the desert without food and water. I'm too old to survive in the wilderness. Have I no value or no right to kind treatment after years of faithful service?*

The stable boy just laughed at the owner's order, thinking that getting rid of the donkey would mean less work for him. "I'll get rid of him for you tomorrow," he said.

The donkey had no place to run, for he needed the security of the stable. He quietly accepted his fate, dreading the thought of starving in the desert. Every hour that passed was agony, baptized by his impending doom.

Morning came as it had every other morning for the donkey, even though it was the day he was to be taken to the desert. The sun rose, and the air was filled with a feast of wonderful odors. Yet all the donkey could smell was his own fear.

Uh-oh! Here comes the stable owner with his stable boy. He's pointing toward me.

"Come on, old boy. Your time is up," said the owner. "You just shouldn't have gotten old. Too bad, you're a faithful old fellow."

Head down and tail limp, the little donkey followed the stable boy out of the stable and into the dusty street. It didn't take long to reach the edge of town. The donkey could see the thinning vegetation and barren wastes ahead.

Suddenly, from the direction of town came a shout, "Hold up there! Stop! Bring the donkey back here." The owner was huffing and puffing up the road, shouting and gesturing frantically.

The stable boy stopped and turned, staring at his master with a face expressing bewilderment and amusement. *What on earth does he want?* thought the laborer. *He never moves that fast unless money is involved.* For a fleeting instant, the worker felt a twinge of fear. *Perhaps the owner has lost money and is coming to accuse me. But, no,* he thought, *he called for the donkey.*

Heading back with the donkey, the stable boy and the owner soon met on the road. "Come on—and be quick about it," said the stable owner. "We have a buyer for the donkey. I think he's a fool, but he said he has just a few denarii and needs a donkey for a trip."

The little donkey was in a daze as he arrived back at the stable. He didn't know what to make of the situation. *A trip? I just hope this person is kind and doesn't push me too hard. I'll try my best for him. Anything is better than the desert.* Thoughts were rushing through the little fellow's head, helter-skelter. Relief and doubt swirled together in his mind, forming a hopeless confusion of thought and feeling.

From behind came a new voice. The little donkey looked back to see a rather tall, lanky fellow approaching. He had a full beard, graying somewhat, and a walk that told of too much bending and standing. The eyes were bright and the wrinkles spread out as a kind of laughter and thoughtfulness. His hands were the hands of a craftsman, but his touch was gentle, even expressed through hard fingers.

"What is his name?" The man, called Joseph, asked the stable owner.

"No name," was the terse reply. "He's a work animal, not a pet."

"Well, he shall have a name," offered Joseph. "Old fellow, what shall I call you? Perhaps . . . yes, I'll call you Boaz. He was one of my favorite relatives, a hardworking, honorable man. Yes, Boaz will do nicely."

I don't like being called "old fellow." I wish he would drop that, thought the donkey. *But anything is better than the desert, and "Boaz" isn't half bad. Joseph seems like a good man, kind and gentle.*

"Come on, Boaz, I'll take you home to meet Mary. I hope you two get along. For you see, old fellow, you're going to have to carry her to Bethlehem."

There he goes again with that "old fellow" stuff. Just stick to "Boaz", if you don't mind. Boy, what a comedown from my past exploits on the trade routes, giving some woman a ride to Bethlehem. But anything is better than starving to death. Leaving the stable was a relief to Boaz, and as the distance increased between the donkey and his previous residence, he began to relax.

Soon, Joseph stopped in front of his workshop and went in. After a few minutes, he came back with a young woman, showing all the signs of carrying a child. "Mary, meet Boaz," said Joseph. "Now, Boaz, you be gentle."

What does he think I'm going to do, bite her on the arm? Boaz was getting some of his donkey spirit back again. After all, they do have a reputation for being a bit feisty at times.

"Caesar Augustus has made our life very difficult by calling for this enrollment," Joseph said to Mary. "The trip to Bethlehem won't be easy, but Boaz seems gentle enough so that you won't have a difficult time."

"Difficult time" he says. If I'm not careful and easy of step, she'll be having that baby on the road.

"Joseph, I'm concerned," commented Mary. "The baby is due anytime, and I fear for the child's life, what with forced travel and no place to stay when we get there. Our midwife can't follow us to Bethlehem."

"I'm worried too, Mary," said Joseph, "but I trust God that all will be well."

I'm glad you trust God, Joseph, but you should also pray that this "old fellow" doesn't drop his load. Boaz was still feeling a bit irritated at all this *old* talk.

Two days after the purchase of Boaz, Joseph and Mary started their perilous journey to Bethlehem. The little donkey very carefully picked his way along the road, gently moving through ruts, stepping lightly over rocks, and avoiding holes.

"What a wonderful donkey I purchased, Mary," observed Joseph, feeling very pleased at this choice.

"Yes, Boaz is very gentle. I've come to love the little fellow," said Mary.

Well, what did you expect? I've never stumbled with a load yet, mused Boaz. *And please drop the mushy stuff. After all, I'm a donkey of worldly experience.*

Late in the day, they arrived at Bethlehem and made the round of inns in the area. Nothing was available except a stable around back of one of the inns. Mary and Joseph found themselves gratefully unloading their meager baggage into the hay. Joseph would have to look for a house later.

Sleep was sound and peaceful until Mary went into labor. "Joseph, Joseph, wake up," came the plea in the night. "I'm in labor. Our child is about to be born."

Boy, was that close! thought Boaz. *We just made it.*

Birth came slowly and with the pain women bear; but finally, a child was safely placed in his mother's arms.

"Joseph, remember the angel's command," said Mary softly. "We shall call him 'Jesus.'"

"Come here, little Jesus," said Joseph. "You are a very special child, called to earth by our heavenly Father."

The little donkey hadn't watched the birth, for he had always been a little queasy. Besides, the hay was fresh, and he was hungry.

Another baby in the world, thought Boaz. *Just listen to them fussing over the child. Frankly, all human babies look the same to me. Now, little donkeys have personality and uniqueness.*

In the early hours of the morning, a shepherd appeared at the stable door. His face was deeply lined by weather and toil. And then, another shepherd and another appeared, followed by several lambs. They saw the baby and fell down on their faces, worshipping God.

"We were visited by angels in the field," said one of the men. "We were told of great things happening. The heavenly host said that the Messiah had been born in Bethlehem. We searched for some time, finally being led to this stable. God be praised! We have seen our King."

Boaz came to attention at the mention of the Messiah. He had heard the stories about an expected King, God's Son. Could it be that he, Boaz, had carried the mother of the Messiah? Surely, God would not have chosen an old donkey to carry the mother of his Son. But as he looked at Joseph and Mary and then at the child, somehow he knew that this Jesus was the Messiah of God. Perhaps God chose him because he needed the slow step of an old, road-wise donkey. At that thought, the little donkey threw his head up and let out a loud donkey guffaw that startled everyone in the stable into laughter and joy.

A Christmas Story

If Jerry enjoyed Main Street on ordinary days, he was ecstatic on this particular evening as he walked along with his grandfather. Christmas was just a week away, and the town was decked out in holiday dress. At the corner of Church Street and Main, the old hotel was beautifully decorated with red-and-green lights in the shape of a Christmas tree that was about ten stories high. Jerry grabbed his grandfather's coat and tugged him to a stop so that they could enjoy the scene.

"Come on, Jerry," urged his granddad. "We have errands to run."

"But look, Granddaddy," the eight-year-old Jerry said breathlessly. "Look at the tree and all the other lights along the street."

"Looks like someone's having a birthday party, Jerry," laughed his grandfather.

Jerry hadn't thought of it that way, for the beautiful decorations had absorbed all of his attention, but he wasted no time on the idea. Everywhere he turned, there was some new scene with flashing lights, tinsel, and snow. In the main window of the town's largest department store was a miniature village with little mechanical people making toys, and they all moved as if strangely alive. So taken was he with the village that Jerry forgot where he was or why he was there.

"Come on, Jerry," said his grandfather, but to no avail.

Jerry thought he heard his name, but couldn't draw his attention from one of the villagers who was working at a cobbler's bench.

"Jerry, come on. You can look later, after we've bought our gifts."

This time Jerry heard his granddaddy and reluctantly obeyed his urging to come. The two friends, for they truly were friends, walked along until they came to a large department store, which boasted Santa's presence; but the pair did not stop at the North Pole, south branch. Jerry had come to buy presents for his family and his best friend Billy. He had worked all summer doing chores and in the fall raking leaves to have enough money for Christmas. Jerry had already picked out the gifts on a previous visit to the store, for he had to be certain that he had enough money. With pockets filled with a few dollar bills and a large amount of change, he got about the joy of buying presents. Jerry's grandfather left him to do shopping of his own with the agreement to meet near Santa Land.

Jerry filled his arms with presents and got in line at the cash register. The store was very crowded, and the checkout line was several people long. Jerry waited patiently until his turn to pay. Depositing his precious cargo on the counter, he began to dig out the money that was stored in several pockets. Out came the few bills and then the quarters, dimes, nickels, and pennies. The clerk added up the purchases and waited on payment. Jerry was carefully counting the money while the clerk became increasingly agitated. "What's the matter with you, kid? Can't you count? You stupid or something?" The clerk kept up the barrage: "When I was in school, they learned us something. Maybe you're just slow!" Some laughter could be heard from the people waiting behind Jerry.

Jerry, who was already shy and self-conscious, suddenly felt small and alone. Never in his young life had anyone called him stupid or slow. Doubts and fears swirled in his mind, and tears welled up in his eyes. Faltering and almost forgetting how much he had counted, Jerry managed to finish and pushed the money toward the clerk. The clerk, looming like a giant, scowled once more and swept away the money, nearly throwing it in the cash register. Jerry wanted to run, but his legs felt stiff and heavy. So he just took his gifts and left the counter, feeling smaller and smaller with each step. Jerry no longer cared about Christmas, gifts, decorations, or people. For the first time in his life, he felt that he didn't belong.

After several minutes of waiting at Santa Land without noticing anything but his own doubt and fear, Jerry felt a hand on his shoulder. Turning, he recognized through his daze the welcome appearance of his granddad. Without thinking about where he was, Jerry hugged his grandfather, tears streaming down his face. Grandfather Martin held his grandson for several seconds and then led him out of the store.

"Jerry, what's the matter? What happened in the store?"

"The clerk at the counter called me 'stupid' and 'slow.'"

"Why do you think he did that?"

"Because I couldn't count the money fast enough."

"I see," said his granddad. "You aren't slow, and you certainly aren't stupid. You are a bright young person."

"Why did he say those things to me? Why?"

"Jerry, the man was probably tired and rushed. Sometimes, we grown-ups speak before we think."

"But, Granddad, what he said hurt me and won't go away."

"Come on, Jerry. Let's walk a bit, and you'll start feeling better."

"I don't feel good. I don't want to walk. Let's go home."

Jerry's granddad knelt down and gave his grandson a big hug. "All right, Jerry, we'll go home."

Jerry and his grandfather retraced their steps down Main Street, but the decorations and the miniature village held no interest for the pair. The happiness of just an hour or so before had been turned to pain. All Jerry could think about was the clerk's face, and he kept hearing the words "slow" and "stupid." Even the joy of buying presents for others had been lost in Jerry's self-doubt.

When the two friends reached Church Street, Jerry's granddad kept going down Main. Now this was unusual, for the shortest way home was down Church to Lindsay Street. Jerry was so lost in thought that he took no notice at first, but about halfway between Church and Willowbrook Streets, he realized the change of routes.

"Granddad, why are we going this way? I want to go home."

"I know, Jerry, but we're only going two blocks out of the way. I thought we would go down to see the nativity scene at the Lutheran Church."

"Why?"

"Well, what happened to you in the store hurt me almost as much as it hurt you. I don't feel good about what we humans do to each other. The Christmas spirit sort of drained out of me, and I need to remember what Christmas is really about."

Silence fell on the pair for the block or so that remained until they stood in front of the crowded display on the church lawn. The nativity scene wasn't professionally made, seeming a bit rough. The figures were cut from plywood and painted, not very well. But there was a lifelike quality about Joseph, Mary, and Jesus. Several minutes had passed when Jerry looked up at his grandfather. His grandfather's face was drawn, lined, and strained.

"Jerry, do you know what Christmas is about?"

"It's about the birth of Jesus in Bethlehem."

"Yes, but do you know who Jesus was and why he came?"

"In Sunday school I learned that he is the savior, but I don't know what that means."

"Christians believe that God came in the man Jesus of Nazareth and that God came to tell all people that he loves us and wants us to love each other."

Jerry was silent, because he didn't understand about God being in Jesus and because he didn't feel good about himself or the man at the store.

Mr. Martin stood, studying Jerry's face for a while, and knew that he hadn't helped much with the explanation.

"Jerry, let me try telling about Jesus in a different way. The part about God's coming in Jesus is impossible for us to understand; rather, it is a matter of faith for Christians. Perhaps I can explain Christmas in this way. The clerk in the store called you names. His word was very important to you because he was a grown-up and had authority. Jesus is God's Word to us and that Word is that he loves us so much that every hair on our heads is numbered and every breath we take is noticed. Our value is beyond measure—no matter what any person says or does to us. Jesus came to tell us that the highest authority in the universe and beyond gives his Word that we are important to him."

"Does he love the clerk at the store?"

"Yes, Jerry, he loves the clerk; and perhaps if the clerk knew how much God loved him, he would have felt better about himself and would not have hurt you this evening. You see, we humans have been hurting each other through history, because we don't know that we are truly loved. We feel bad about ourselves, and we lash out at others to make them feel bad. Perhaps the fellow at the store was called stupid and slow when he was a boy and never knew the truth of God's love and his own personal value."

"I'm sorry if someone called him stupid. It hurts, Granddad."

"I know, Jerry. The hurt will pass if you remember how much you are loved by God and by your family, and we can pray that the fellow at the store will discover the meaning of Christmas and stop hurting."

"Granddad, I'm cold. Let's go home and get some hot chocolate."

As Jerry and his grandfather turned to leave, Jerry whispered, "Happy birthday, Jesus."

Christmas Eve, 1933

Jarrett pressed his nose against the toy store window and watched with rapt attention the train that raced around the tracks. The engine was a tin replica of a mountain steam engine, and it pulled several cars. One of the cars was filled with milk cans, another with telephone poles, and another with coal. The caboose was bright red and had a conductor standing on the rear platform. A store employee, who saw the little boy watching, stopped by the display to couple and uncouple the cars, making Jarrett's eyes so wide that they seemed a misfit for his thin face. Jarrett was so taken by the display that he neither felt the cold nor heard his mother's voice as she approached to walk him home.

"Let's go, Jarrett. I've finished shopping, and we need to get home for supper. Besides, you must be freezing. Do you hear me?"

"Oh, hello, Mom. I really like that train in the window," Jarrett's voice had a plaintive quality.

"Son, you know that I don't have the money to buy the train for you. How I would like to, but I can't," said his mom with a sad but firm reply.

Jarrett heard the pain in his mother's voice and said nothing. *After all,* he thought, *she would buy the train if she could but* . . . Tears filled his eyes as he remembered last Christmas. Jarrett took his mother's hand in his and moved as close as he could to her love and warmth as they made their way home.

The Great Depression had settled like a death shroud over America, making life hard and bitter for millions of families. Jarrett's family was no exception. Jarrett's mind wandered over the memory of a world globe he saw at school, and he wondered if other children and families were experiencing the same depression. What had made things much more difficult was that his father had lost his job at the local furniture factory very soon after the stock market crash. Unable to find a comparable job, Jarrett's dad had supported the family by doing odd jobs, running errands, hauling wood and coal, and doing anything, no matter how hard, dangerous, or degrading. For three years, the family had scarcely scraped by, living in a cold-water flat on meager rations. Jarrett watched his dad come in at night so exhausted that he couldn't stay awake at the supper table and growing thinner day by day. And just when things seemed to be as bad as they could be, Jarrett's dad died of pneumonia on Christmas Eve, 1932. Jarrett's mom was fortunate to have a job as a domestic for a rich family living in Emerywood Estates. The pay was inadequate, but it put food on the table and kept a roof over their heads.

As Jarrett walked along with his mom, he began to recall last Christmas Eve. His father had developed a severe cold and cough a week before he died. On Christmas Eve, the doctor came to treat his dad, who could barely breathe and was burning with fever. Jarrett sat at his father's side all afternoon and into the evening, holding his father's hand and praying to Jesus to make him well. He could still recall his father's racking cough and feel the burning heat of his fever. Jarrett rubbed his hands as if to rid himself of the sensation and moved closer to his mom as they walked in the cold. He shuddered as he remembered his father's last attempts to breathe and began to cry as he recalled the doctor's gentle but devastating death announcement. Jarrett could still see himself run from the bedroom and out the front door into the snow, and he felt the anger generated by his father's dying and the anger reserved for Jesus for allowing it to happen. Standing in the snow, the little boy wept and threw up his small, bony fist toward heaven in protest and defiance of a Jesus who could take his father. Recovering the present, Jarrett looked up at his mom as they continued toward home and suddenly became afraid that Jesus would take his mom too. What would happen to him, for he would be alone? Jesus didn't seem to care about such things.

As Christmas approached, Jarrett became more and more depressed and angry. His mother tried repeatedly to break through a thickening wall that surrounded him, but to no avail. "Jarrett, please talk to me about how you are feeling. I know that this is a sad time for both of us, but we have to talk about it."

"I don't want to talk. Just leave me alone."

"Please, son, talk to me," his mom spoke softly, holding out her arms ready to receive him. But Jarrett stood rigidly and coldly separate, even though his broken heart needed the healing of his mother's love. After standing in front of his mother for what seemed forever, he could not bring himself to scale the Everest between them; so he turned and left the room.

Jarrett's mom slowly lowered her arms and with her apron wiped her eyes. She was losing her son to grief and knew no way to relieve his pain.

Jarrett refused a part in the Christmas pageant with a silence that would split granite. Church members who had relied upon his participation could not understand his cold rejection. They cajoled, pleaded, and lectured him; but nothing moved his heart. Even the pastor got involved, but quickly realized that his persuasion was unwelcome and useless.

Christmas Eve arrived with cold and snow, not that they weren't already present in Jarrett's heart.

"Jarrett, come on. We're going to be late for the service," called his mom.

"I'm not going to church, especially on Jesus' birthday," shot back Jarrett.

"Son, we've never missed a Christmas Eve service, well . . . except for last Christmas. I want to go and be with the church. They have been kind and helpful to us since your father's death. Besides, this is a holy night, the night of Christ's birth. Let's go to worship."

With an explosion of pain, anger, and grief, Jarrett's emotional dam broke, flooding the room with a bitter attack upon his father and Jesus. "How could my dad die and leave us in this poverty, leave me without a father, leave you, Mom, with no help? I hate him! Do you hear me? I hate him! And that Jesus I was taught to love, how can I worship *Him?* How can I worship the one who allowed my father to die?" Jarrett stood rigidly in place and continued to shout through angry sobs. His mom was speechless at what was pouring out of her son. She had no idea that he felt such deep anger toward his dad or Jesus. Her mouth hung open as if she had had been hit in the stomach, and her feet seemed nailed to the floor. She could do nothing but stare at her son.

Jarrett dropped to his knees and wept. After a time, his mom knelt beside him and put an arm around him and quietly cried with him. Gradually, he melted into her arms and became limp and still.

"Your father loved us so much that he worked himself to death just trying to keep us together, fed, clothed, and sheltered. He was a good and faithful man who fought for our very lives up to his last breath. Do you really think he wanted to leave us behind, to desert us? Surely, Jarrett, you can't believe such a thing about your father."

"Mom, I know he loved us and didn't want to die. It's just that I need him so . . . I, I loved him so much that his absence is a large lump in my throat that won't go away. And I'm afraid that you're going to die too. Mom, I'm so afraid."

"Jarrett, I'm here, and I love you. I'm not going anywhere," said his mother, holding her son's face gently in her hands. "No, I can't know what the future holds; but we are together, and we love each other. Let's be thankful for that and be thankful for the love we received from your father. Let's not be angry at his death. In fact, the reason we—yes, I said *we*—got angry at your father is that he was so special, and we lost so much."

"You've been angry at Dad?" asked Jarrett with a shocked expression.

"Yes, son, I too resented your father for leaving us; but it was because I loved him so much, and he had loved us so much. Only those who have much to lose suffer the greatest pain."

"I'm so sorry, Mom, for not talking to you. I've been so hurt that I didn't think about your pain."

"Jarrett, we've both closed ourselves up in cocoons of grief, and we haven't been as caring as we should. Now that the cocoons have split open, maybe we can start a new life," said his mom with a momentary thaw of her own pain. "Why don't we wash our faces and go to church."

"Mom, I'm still mad at Jesus. He didn't have to let Dad die!"

"Jarrett, it's not Jesus' fault that your father died. He doesn't steal our loved ones from us or punish us by hurting others. Jesus loves us and has made a good, warm, loving place for your father. Come on. Let's go to church."

Mother and son walked slowly to the church through deep snow and listened to the joyous sounds of church bells on the cold, night air. Jarrett loved to hear the bells, but tonight it was not the same, for Jarrett had pushed Jesus away.

The church was filled with people, and the decorations were beautiful. On the dais was the nativity scene with a beautiful glass star shining brightly above it. All the candles of the Advent wreath were lighted, including the large Christ candle. The choir was decked out in Christmas robes, and the pastor was wearing a black robe and a beautiful white stole reaching down to his knees. To the right of the dais was a large Christmas tree decorated with Christian symbols and covered with white lights. Wreaths ringed the sanctuary, and the organist played Vivaldi's "Gloria."

The choir was wonderfully prepared and gave a beautiful Christmas concert, followed by the pastor's Christmas message. Jarrett listened as the pastor told the story of Jesus' birth and life as was the custom, but the pastor added a special note to the story when he spoke of the likelihood of Joseph's death and Jesus' shouldering of the family responsibilities. He went on to say how much Jesus must have missed his dad, but that Jesus faithfully lived his life to honor his earthly father and the heavenly Father. Jarrett thought that the pastor spoke right to him when he said, "Jesus suffered his own losses in life just as we do and, therefore, understands our suffering." Jarrett sat listening, stunned by what he was hearing. Jesus lost his father too and understands what I am feeling. The young boy, would-be young man, began to pray: "Dear Jesus, I didn't know that your father died and left you to go on without him. I'm sorry for you, for it hurts a lot, doesn't it? Please help me to be the man of the house and to help my mother. She's hurt too. Jesus, I know that you didn't take my father, for you wouldn't do that, knowing how much it hurts. Forgive me for being so mad at you, but you understand."

When mother and son reached home, she rushed her son off to bed so that she could finish some Christmas baking. Jarrett's mom had carefully saved sugar, spices, and flour to make cake and cookies for her son's present. There was no money for anything else. She worked all night and finished by wrapping the Christmas goodies in brown paper from grocery bags. Jarrett finally dozed off with the smell of gingerbread filling the house and his dreams.

Christmas morning dawned bright and beautiful, the kind of scene found on a Currier & Ives plate. Jarrett was the first out of bed, but he waited patiently for his mother to wake up. Under the little cedar, there were several boxes with his name on them. His mind briefly took him back to the toy store and that beautiful, fast locomotive, but he knew that there would be no train this year. Somehow, it didn't seem to matter, for the emptiness in his heart had been replaced by a feeling of peace and love.

"Open your presents," came the word from his mom. Jarrett didn't hesitate for a second and tore into his gifts. There he found cookies, divinity candy, and gingerbread, which he eagerly began stuffing into his mouth.

"Jarrett, for goodness sake, slow down. You'll choke," laughed his mom. Jarrett sat staring at her with gingerbread crumbs defining his lips and covering his pajamas. He mumbled something that brought an explosion of cookies pieces from his mouth and simultaneously reached for a piece of divinity candy.

The young lad put down his presents, swallowed, and gave his mother a big hug. He thanked his mom for the gifts. His mother tried to explain that she just couldn't afford the train he wanted, but Jarrett didn't let her finish. He kissed his mother and offered her a piece of candy, which she took with only a mild protest.

"Mom, I miss Dad. I miss him very much," said Jarrett quietly.

"I do too, son. But with the help of Jesus, we'll make it."

Jarrett spotted a cookie hiding under the gingerbread and stuffed the whole thing in his mouth. After all, it was Christmas.

———✦———

The Cedar

Standing in front of 406 Lindsay Street on a cold, gray December morning isn't the smartest thing I've done lately; but here I stand, hands in pockets, collar pulled up, and my head pulled down as far as it will go. How could they have torn down my grandparents' beautiful clapboard house and replaced it with a cracker-box building that houses an insurance office? I wish I had a bulldozer. I'd get rid of this eyesore, post-haste. But, alas, that wouldn't bring back the twelve-room home I played in as a child, nor would it bring back my beloved grandfather.

That wonderful old man smelled of cigars and plowed earth and carried on his clothes the undeniable signs of hard manual labor. He had great strength and extraordinary physical courage. I used to chin on his extended right arm and walk with him, without fear, through herds of large farm animals. His theory of boy-rearing was that boys are kept out of trouble by hard work. Granddad convinced me that slopping hogs was fun, instead of hard work; and you know, he was right! What great times I had feeding the hogs and watching their antics at the trough, not unlike a growing boy at the dinner table; but mucking out the pens was a different matter. Not only was it hard work, but also hogs pay little attention to a kid who weighs less than an eighth of their heft. They stepped on my toes, knocked me down, and generally pushed me about the pen. Mother dreaded to see me after a day with the pigs. Try as she would, my clothes didn't come clean, and the odor of muck was permanent. Grandfather gave little heed to my mom's complaints and kept me busy with all sorts of wonderful messy chores. I can still see him rolling on the ground with laughter at my first attempt to plow behind a horse. I used every word Grandfather taught me to control that horse, but the horse took one look at me and completely ignored my orders. The horse and I plowed right out of the field and into the neighbor's adjoining backyard.

My grandparents were Methodists and attended South Main Street Methodist Church. Grandmother was really a Wesleyan Methodist, but my grandfather considered that religious fanaticism. He regularly thwarted Grandmother's attempts to draw him into her piety by telling jokes and stories that loosened the bun of hair, which was tightly wound on the back of her head. He also drank corn whiskey for *cough syrup*. According to my grandfather, that was easier than using whiskey for snake-bite medicine; because that would mean having to carry a snake with him, and he didn't like snakes. Other than these occasional excursions into sin to needle my grandmother, he was a true Methodist and believed in discipline for his favorite grandson. He never abused me, but I felt the sting of the switch and the pop of the razor strap. On the whole, I received a lot less punishment than I deserved, but that's another story.

I lost my granddad to cancer when I was twelve and he was seventy-two. I practically lived with my grandparents during his illness and witnessed his courage and determination. During the entire time of his decline from great physical prowess to emaciation, he stayed active, refusing to be bedridden for any length of time. I can't remember the funeral, and I really don't know why. I suppose that I never believed he would die.

The cold is making my eyes water as I look around for remnants of my past. Through the tears, I can see the huge boulders in the alley at the rear of the property. My friends and I shot a million bad guys from behind those rocks, pretending to be Roy Rogers, Gene Autry, and Rocky Lane. The old magnolia tree with its hard-to-rake leaves is gone. We used its seedpods for hand grenades. Only a part of the hedge that I loved to hate is still standing. During growing season, many of my Saturdays were spent trimming the hedge and being bitten by bugs that made their home there. Other than these things, not much is left on the property to tug at my memory.

Wait a minute! Wait . . . a . . . minute! Could it be? Could that be the cedar tree that my grandfather and I planted at Christmas many years ago? It must be! Look at the size of that tree and its perfect shape. Who would've thought the little cedar we planted would become such a tall, handsome tree. Touching and smelling these branches floods my mind with the memory of a very special Christmas.

Every Christmas, my grandfather and I went out to the farm on Kivett Drive and cut a cedar. Cedars were plentiful on the farm and had to be thinned out from time to time, so we would cut down a nicely shaped tree for the living room. The room was spacious and cool, so a tree kept its freshness for weeks. The Christmas of special memory was unusual for several reasons. We had an early snow, and that was unusual for North Carolina. I tramped through the patches of snow, making loud crunching noises and feeling like a young pioneer. We took longer than usual to find a suitable tree, even though there were plenty of beautiful trees to choose from. It was as if we had to find one special tree. When we found just the right tree, Granddad started to chop it down; but on impulse, I intervened. "Let's not cut this one down. Let's dig it up and plant it after Christmas." We had never done this before, and I'm not sure why I said what I did.

"Don't believe it'll live," responded a slightly bewildered Granddad.

"But can't we try? Just think of it planted in the front yard," I pleaded.

"Don't have room for another tree in the front yard. We got a big magnolia and a maple already," reminded Granddad. "But maybe we can put it in the backyard."

"No, not in the backyard, in the front," I responded. Normally, I would have respectfully accepted my grandfather's judgment, but this was important to me for reasons I did not understand.

"Got no room in the front, and a tree can't grow without plenty of room, just like a boy," observed my grandfather.

"Please, Granddaddy. Let me plant the tree after Christmas!"

"Go get the shovel out of the car, and we'll dig it up," he said, shaking his head.

"Yippee," I shouted, as I ran toward the old Hudson.

We dug up the cedar and wrapped the roots with burlap bags that we kept in the farm shed and tied the tree on top of the car. What a sight we must have been. The hand-painted black Hudson, with a texture of bottomland and hauling a cedar on top, must have looked like rolling moss. My grandmother thought the whole thing funny, until we left a trail of dirt in the living room. She had a neat fit and ordered us out of the house. But after pleading with her, she gave in and let me decorate the little cedar.

Grandmother didn't have an abundance of decorations, only a couple of strings of lights, some icicles, a few colored glass balls, and some cranberry and paper chains that we made. Frankly, the tree wasn't the prettiest tree I've ever seen; it was rather bare. But the beauty of this tree was in the relationship with my grandfather and the prospect of planting the tree together. It was then, as it is now, a living symbol of love between two people.

After the Christmas gathering, Granddad and I planted the tree at the end of the front porch next to Mrs. Stiles's property. The location was carefully chosen for the cedar's benefit and so that I could keep watch over our tree from my room. I was faithful to attend the tree for awhile, but as with most of us, I soon forgot. Every once in a while, I would give some thought to the tree, but for the most part the oversight gave way to thoughtlessness.

But as with most things planted by love, the tree kept growing; and on this cold December morning, it reminded me of a loving grandfather, plowed earth, cigars, a hand-painted Hudson, slopping hogs, and a rugged hand, gently holding mine as I tried to keep up. The cedar was and remains a symbol of unbroken love.

As I stand here looking at a Christmas tree that tells the story of the love between grandfather and grandson, I know that every Christmas, trees tell the story of an even greater, deeper love: God's love for his children. Evergreen Christmas trees speak of life, and the decorations tell of the one who gives it; and, with a little reflection, we can imagine another tree planted on a lonely hill outside of Jerusalem, a place called Golgotha. This tree bore the dying Son of God, soaked up his blood, shivered with the motion of his writhing body, and felt, with all creation, the moment of the Creator's death. O, Lord, let us see past the piles of presents this Christmas to the tree and discover the symbol of eternal love. And when we forget the meaning of Christmas, as we are wont to do, give your Holy Spirit to our wayward hearts, so that we can recall the divine gift of your Son and the tree on which he died.

I wonder how long I've been here. My family will be concerned about my absence. After all, we're here for this year's Christmas gathering, and I don't want to miss the fun. Just one more look at 406 Lindsay Street and the cedar tree. I think I'll break off a small branch for my son and daughter. Perhaps they'll like the story and find some value in it. I hope that I can leave a symbol of love for my children and grandchildren, like a cedar Christmas tree.

Well, Granddad, I'll meet you at the tree. I love you.

---

www.ingramcontent.com/pod-product-compliance
Ingram Content Group UK Ltd.
Pitfield, Milton Keynes, MK11 3LW, UK
UKHW041307191025
8470UKWH00023B/158